A Student's
to Rab

STUDENT GUIDES TO EUROPEAN LITERATURE

General Editor: Brian Masters
Molière, by Brian Masters
Sartre, by Brian Masters
Goethe, by F. J. Lamport
Rabelais, by Brian Masters
Corneille, by J. H. Broome
Böll, by Enid Macpherson

A Student's Guide To Rabelais

by
BRIAN MASTERS

HEINEMANN EDUCATIONAL
BOOKS LTD · LONDON

Heinemann Educational Books Ltd
LONDON EDINBURGH MELBOURNE
SINGAPORE JOHANNESBURG
NEW DELHI TORONTO AUCKLAND
HONG KONG NAIROBI
IBADAN

ISBN 0 435 37574 1

© Brian Masters 1971
First published 1971

Published by
Heinemann Educational Books Ltd
48 Charles Street, London W1X 8AH
Printed in Great Britain by
Cox and Wyman Ltd, London, Fakenham and Reading

Contents

Foreword	ix
Acknowledgements	x
Chapter One: BIOGRAPHICAL INTRODUCTION	1
Chapter Two: THE RENAISSANCE IN FRANCE	13
Chapter Three: THE HUMANISM OF RABELAIS	23
Chapter Four: ON EDUCATION	32
Chapter Five: LES PETITS MOYNETONS	41
Chapter Six: ON RELIGION	46
Chapter Seven: THE NATURALISM OF RABELAIS: L'ABBAYE DE THÉLÈME	70
Chapter Eight: ON AGGRESSION	78
Chapter Nine: THE MEDIEVAL LEGACY	87
Chapter Ten: SOME PORTRAITS AND OPINIONS	98
Bibliography	109

To Kenneth

Foreword

This book is intended for the use of students approaching Rabelais for the first time. It attempts to give a brief introduction, concentrating on the main recurrent themes, and to point the way towards further study. The reader's attention is drawn to the various controversies which surround the interpretation of Rabelais's ideas; for a fuller analysis of the questions raised, the student is referred to works listed in the bibliography.

Quotations from Rabelais are taken from the *Bibliothèque de la Pléiade* edition of the complete works, which is based on the 1542 text of *Gargantua and Pantagruel*, and on the 1552 text of the *Tiers Livre* and the *Quart Livre,* incorporating the amendments made by Rabelais. For the spelling, I have followed that used in the Pléiade edition, maintaining the final *z* instead of *s* in the plural, but adding modern French accents wherever they facilitate an understanding of the text.

Rabelais presents a peculiar difficulty to the student unaquainted with sixteenth-century syntax and vocabulary. We have therefore decided to depart from the general policy applied to French books in this series, and to offer translations of quotations. Translations are taken from the J. M. Cohen version published by Penguin Books.

Wynyard, 1970

Acknowledgements

I should like to offer my gratitude to Penguin Books Ltd., who have kindly allowed their translation of *Gargantua and Pantagruel* by J. M. Cohen to be used in this essay.

E. K. Timings Esq. has been most kind and helpful with suggestions, which I am anxious to acknowledge, and my thanks are also due to Alistair Londonderry, without whose generous hospitality and support this book would have been considerably more difficult to write.

1
Biographical Introduction

Until the early part of this century, a firm tradition held that François Rabelais was the poor peasant son of an innkeeper, and that his entire life was spent in a state of inebriety. He was said to have written bawdy stories in a haze of intoxication after long nights of debauch and abandon. Rabelais himself contributed to the legend in his lifetime, and was echoed by his contemporaries soon after his death. Ronsard wrote his epitaph:

> Au bon Rabelais qui boivoit
> Tousjours, cependant qu'il vivoit.

It was then a simple matter for the legend to assume the dignity of fact, and for literary historians to lose sight of the real man behind the caricature. For caricature it is. Rabelais was in fact an academic of immense learning and erudition, whose knowledge was encyclopaedic and never satiated, who wrote in Latin and Greek as well as French, and who was counted among the six best doctors of his age. His contemporary Étienne Dolet called him 'l'honneur et gloire de la médicine'.

Nobody knows precisely when François Rabelais was born. It is doubtful whether Rabelais knew himself, since little attention was paid to such details in those days. One tends now to accept the date offered by Abel Lefranc, 4 February, 1494. But even this precision is the result only of very clever guesswork, and has recently been challenged.

Modern research has shown that François's father, Antoine

Rabelais, was not an innkeeper, but an eminent lawyer and landowner of bourgeois stock. A wealthy and respected personage, he held various properties in and around Chinon, including a small farmhouse called La Devinière, where his fourth child and third son, François, was born. The farmhouse can be seen to this day.

The early years of François Rabelais are a mystery. It is likely that he was educated at the Benedictine Abbey of Seuilly, nearby, and then at the Franciscan monastery La Baumette. He may also have studied at the University of Angers. Whatever the case, we find him in 1520 wearing the robes of a Franciscan friar at Fontenay-le-Comte, where he became very friendly with a prominent Hellenist, Pierre Amy. With Amy's encouragement, Rabelais taught himself Greek (no mean accomplishment in France in 1520, where there were no teachers of Greek and textbooks had to be imported from Italy), wrote to the foremost French scholar of the time, Guillaume Budé, and attempted to translate Herodotus. One of his letters to Budé survives. He also met the lawyer, writer and Humanist André Tiraqueau. It is fair to say that Rabelais's leanings towards Humanism date from this period.

The Faculty of Theology at the University of Paris, commonly called La Sorbonne, had banned the study of Greek as being likely to lead to heresy. Rabelais's and Amy's Greek texts were therefore confiscated, and the two friends parted company. Rabelais went to the Benedictine monastery of Maillezais (with the special permission of the Pope), where intellectual research was more easily tolerated. His books were eventually restored to him, probably due to the intervention of the Bishop of Maillezais, Geoffroy d'Estissac, himself a Humanist. The next three years were extremely relaxed and happy for Rabelais. Geoffrey d'Estissac appointed him teacher to his nephew, and made him his secretary. As such, he travelled widely in France, extended his acquaintance with men of letters, broadened his experience in Hellenic studies, apparently without any of the

BIOGRAPHICAL INTRODUCTION

censorship previously imposed by the Franciscans, and made himself known as a bright young scholar. He probably attended lectures at the University of Poitiers during this period of maturing scholarship.

In 1528 Rabelais discarded his monk's habit to become, like Erasmus, a secular priest. It is doubtful whether we shall ever know what prompted this important decision, though it may have been a desire to study medicine. During the following two years, Rabelais was at the universities of Bordeaux, Toulouse, Orléans, and Paris. Finally, in 1530, he registered on the list of students at the famous Faculty of Medicine of the University of Montpellier, and six weeks after the start of his courses, he matriculated as Bachelor of Medicine. Clearly, he must have been a student of medicine long before going to Montpellier, and his reputation as a doctor must have preceded him. As a graduate, Rabelais had to give a public course; his subjects were Hippocrates and Galen and, unlike his predecessors, he worked directly from the original Greek texts, rather than from poor Latin translations. His classes were always packed.

Surprisingly, Rabelais did not stay at Montpellier to continue medical studies, but went instead to Lyon. This was to be a move of singular importance, since Lyon then had more claims to being the cultural centre of France than did Paris. Here were all the more important publishers and the literary fairs famous throughout Europe. It was in Lyon that the literary sophisticates assembled, the scholars and the men of letters. Moreover, its proximity to Italy meant that Lyon was close to the heart of the Renaissance influence which was being strongly felt in France around 1530. It is little wonder, then, that Rabelais, now learned in law and medicine as well as Classical literatures, should choose Lyon as his centre at this time. Between 1530 and 1534 he lived in a climate of exciting intellectual activity, met the most famous writers and poets of his day, including Dolet and Bonaventure des Périers, and published the works which were to establish his renown throughout Europe. On

1 November 1532, he was appointed doctor at the Hospital of Notre-Dame de Pitié, although he was still technically only a Bachelor of Medicine.

1532 is a year of cardinal importance for Rabelais, the year in which he ceased to be a peripheral character in literary circles and published books of his own. At the beginning of the year, he edited a collection of letters, in Latin, by the Italian doctor Giovanni Manardi, with a Preface in which he set forth his own ideas on the teaching of medicine, emphasizing the need to study medical texts in the original. The book was dedicated to his friend André Tiraqueau. Later, an edition of the *Aphorisms* of Hippocrates appeared, with a commentary by Rabelais based on the Greek text which he had used for the course of lectures he had given in Montpellier; this was dedicated to Geoffrey d'Estissac. There followed an edition of the fifteenth-century parody *Testament de Cuspidius*, which Rabelais dedicated to Amaury Bouchard. In this same year, Rabelais made the acquaintance of the secretary to the most revered Humanist in Europe, Erasmus. In a letter which has come down to us (the original of which was composed in Latin), he speaks in glowing terms of Erasmus' influence on his intellectual development; it is a letter which expresses gratitude and admiration in equal measure:

> ... j'ai saisi l'occasion, mon père très bon, de te témoigner par un service quels sentiments, quelle piété j'ai à ton égard. Je t'ai nommé mon père; je devrais dire ma mère, si ton indulgence me le permettait, car, ce qui arrive chaque jour aux femmes qui nourrissent le fruit de leur ventre sans l'avoir jamais vu, qui le protègent des injures de l'air, cela t'est arrivé à toi aussi qui, sans me connaître de vue, sans même savoir mon nom, m'as éduqué, m'as nourri des mamelles très pures de ta science divine, si bien que je ne te rends pas grâce à toi seul de ce que je suis et de ce que je vaux, je serais le plus ingrat de tous les hommes.

BIOGRAPHICAL INTRODUCTION

There was a very popular little book, of uncertain authorship, being widely read in Lyon at this time, called *Les Grandes Chroniques du Grand et Énorme Géant Gargantua*. Rabelais noted, somewhat ruefully, that although the book was not as weighty as the serious medical works he had himself written, 'il en a esté plus vendu par les imprimeurs en deux moys qu'il ne sera acheté de Bibles en neuf ans'. (Prologue to *Pantagruel*.) He decided, then, that since his medical post afforded him only a small salary, and his books were hardly best-sellers, he would write 'un aultre livre de mesme billon', and see if he could not achieve the same degree of popular success. He chose as his subject another giant, the son of Gargantua, and called him Pantagruel. *Les Horribles et Espoventables Faictz et Prouesses du très renommé Pantagruel, Roi des Dipsodes,* were published at the Lyon fair on 3 November 1532. They had been quite possibly written in the space of a few weeks. Their author was Alcofribas Nasier, which is a fairly obvious anagram on François Rabelais. It would be interesting to know if anybody was fooled by this device, but it is easy to understand why the author, a respected doctor and author of medical treatises, should seek the protection of some degree of anonymity. Besides, the book was not merely the amusing and ridiculous adventure story that it pretended to be; it contained some very strong satirical attacks against the Sorbonne which, from its distant seat in Paris, still exercised considerable power.

Since *Pantagruel* is the second in sequence of Rabelais's five books, *Gargantua* being the first, it was for long assumed that they were published in this order. Abel Lefranc and his team have proven, however, that *Pantagruel* was conceived, written and published two years before *Gargantua*. Why choose the name Pantagruel? It was certainly not an invention. In folklore, Pantagruel was a little sea-devil who personified Thirst and whose principal activity was to throw salt into the mouths of drunkards. As there had been a severe drought in France in 1532, lasting several months, the subject of thirst and the name of Pantagruel must have been topics of almost daily conversation. Rabelais made him a giant in order to satisfy popular taste and to earn for himself some of the success which the *Grandes Chroniques* had achieved. He was not wrong in his anticipations: six editions of *Pantagruel* were published between 1532 and 1534.

Pantagruel tells the story of the extraordinary birth, childhood and early manhood of a giant, of his fantastic appetite and astonishing feats, and of his equally mischievous but apparently normal-size friend Panurge. It is a book intended to make the reader laugh aloud, and it succeeds triumphantly. But mingled with the folklore and the outrageous obscenities were pages whose content was manifestly serious, where burning topics relating to religion, politics and education were discussed in a manner which was soon to incur the wrath of the Establishment. There was the unmistakable tone of a crusading Humanist, particularly in passages where the Sorbonne was mercilessly teased. Predictably, the Sorbonne banned the book in 1533 for 'obscenity', a word which then implied 'morally and politically dangerous' rather than 'indecent'. But Rabelais's popularity was henceforth assured.

In January 1533, only two months after the appearance of *Pantagruel*, Rabelais published *La Pantagruéline Prognostication* (again signed by Alcofribas Nasier), a satire on the astrological predictions then very much in vogue, in which he took the opportunity to re-assert his religious integrity.

Meanwhile, Rabelais had acquired a new patron, more powerful even than Geoffroy d'Estissac. This was Jean du Bellay, Bishop of Paris, later to be Cardinal. Du Bellay went to Rome as special envoy of François 1er, and, passing through Lyon, asked Rabelais to accompany him as his personal doctor. It is not difficult to imagine with what eagerness Rabelais accepted the chance to visit Italy, the source of the Renaissance and, for all Humanists, the centre of the intellectual world. Du Bellay and his doctor arrived in Rome in January 1534, and

BIOGRAPHICAL INTRODUCTION

stayed until April. Rabelais spent much of his time in botanical research, but with little result, as he tells us in a letter. He also met some distinguished Italian Humanists and enjoyed the atmosphere of lively academic discovery. On his return to Lyon, he resumed his post at the hospital.

During the summer of 1534 Rabelais wrote his *Gargantua*, which may have appeared at the Book Fair in Lyon in November of that year, although the precise date is still contested. Again he was not aiming at a 'succès d'estime' so much as writing for financial gain. He hoped to repeat the immense popular success of his *Pantagruel*. The story was similar. The giant Gargantua, Pantagruel's father, after an extraordinary birth through his mother's ear, grows into a fine young man, a model of virtue and an ideal of the Renaissance 'uomo universale', defends his father Grandgousier's lands against aggression, befriends a mischievous monk, Frère Jean, and founds a monastery dedicated to Humanist ideals. This is the famous Abbaye de Thélème, about which more later. The book is larded with riotous anecdotes, wondrous tales and broad humour, but the serious content is even more marked than in *Pantagruel*. The chapters dealing with Gargantua's education, with the Picrocholine War, and with Thélème, expound Rabelais's ideas in a tone which is clearly meant to be taken very seriously, while the references to monastic life and to the Sorbonne cry out with fierce anger and sparkling derision. The hostility shown by the Sorbonne against *Pantagruel*, far from subduing Rabelais, has sharpened his determination to attack.

It is worth noting, at this point, that Rabelais rarely if ever showed any bitterness or resentment in his attacks against the Establishment. His satire was all the more potent and irresistible for being good-natured. Certainly, he despised many of the traditions which the Sorbonne held dear, but his tone is one of ribald mockery and derision rather than bitter hatred. It was with reason that Ronsard, in the epitaph quoted above, referred to 'le *bon* Rabelais'.

The ostensible subject of *Gargantua* was taken, in the first instance, from the anonymous *Grandes Chroniques* published in 1532. But the legend of Gargantua was well-known in folklore at least sixty years before this date. The name of *Gargantua* was as common then as Tom Thumb might be now.

It can have been no surprise to anyone that *Gargantua* was condemned by the Sorbonne as 'heretical', especially since its publication had been preceded, only a few weeks earlier, by the notorious 'affaire des placards'. During the night of 17 October 1534, posters appeared all over Paris, and even on the door to the King's bedroom, attacking church services, the cardinals, the Pope. They were an overt challenge to authority and could not be tolerated. The Sorbonne took immediate revenge against the 'heresy' by instigating a wave of persecution. When *Gargantua* appeared in November, with its many pages of joyous irreverence, it was no longer safe for Rabelais (still thinly protected by his anagram) to remain in Lyon. He left in February 1535, probably to stay with Geoffroy d'Estissac, and returned after a few months, when the fear of persecution had subsided. Meanwhile, writers and publishers had been arrested, some had even been burnt at the stake.

Rabelais's literary activity then entered a period of prudent abeyance. He spent most of 1535 in Italy with Cardinal du Bellay, returning to Lyon in 1536. In 1537 he was again in Montpellier, where he took a further degree in medicine, and six weeks later, his Doctorate; now he had full claim to the style of 'Doctor' which he had used for the past five years. In the summer of that year, Rabelais gave a demonstration of anatomy by dissecting the body of a hanged man, and was thus one of the first doctors to do so in France. In the autumn, he gave another lecture on Hippocrates in Montpellier, basing his commentary once again on the original Greek text.

In July, 1538, Rabelais was present at the meeting between Francois 1er and the Emperor Charles V at Aigues-Mortes. He returned to Lyon with the King's entourage. Already for some years an intimate of Vatican politics, he became ever more closely accepted in the King's company, and was later to undertake official duties on the King's instructions.

At the end of 1539, Rabelais went to Italy for the third time, on this occasion with Guillaume du Bellay, Seigneur de Langey, brother to the cardinal. He appears to have remained in Italy for a long period, returning to Lyon in 1542 to publish new editions of *Gargantua* and *Pantagruel* to which he made various amendments, excising the more blatantly dangerous satires. It is this final edition that I have used for the purpose of this essay. The new editions were condemned for the third time by the highest religious authority in the land (on 2 March 1543), a fact which does not seem to have hindered their author's progress in the royal favour. Dolet had brought out reprints of the original versions only a few months before, without of course any of Rabelais's amendments to the text. The author disclaims any responsibility for these pirate editions in his preface; indeed, he seizes more than one opportunity to aver his nationalism and his loyalty to the King.

On 9 January 1543, Guillaume du Bellay died in the presence of Rabelais, who thereby lost a dear friend and a powerful protector. Shortly afterwards, the death also occurred of Geoffroy d'Estissac. What became of Rabelais in the next two years is not clear; in the absence of any evidence to the contrary, one assumes that he continued his medical duties in Lyon. We know also that he was appointed 'maître des requêtes' by the King, and that in 1545 he obtained the rare privilege of a Royal Licence to publish new editions of his first two books, and to cover any future works for the next six years. This unusual display of royal favour and protection was almost an insult to the Sorbonne doctors, who had relentlessly pursued Rabelais for twelve years, and it enabled Rabelais to write under his own name for the first time, When the *Tiers Livre* appeared in 1546, it was signed by Doctor François Rabelais. It is dedicated to the

King's sister, Marguerite de Navarre, an authoress in her own right.

The *Tiers Livre* purports to continue the story of Pantagruel and Panurge, but in fact the bulk of the book is more in the manner of a treatise than a narrative. The question at issue is whether or not Panurge should marry. Well over two-thirds of the book are devoted to a discussion of the problem. Various authorities are consulted and a variety of views are aired. With the *Tiers Livre* Rabelais has clearly decided to play safe, to enter a discussion which was very fashionable and fairly harmless, on the nature and value of women. Although there are amusing anecdotes, there are none of the dangerously accurate satires against the Faculty of Theology which had characterized *Gargantua* and *Pantagruel*. It is a mature work, the product of a lifetime of scholarship. The display of knowledge, literary, juridical, theological, economical, is simply staggering, the number of classical references amazing.

Nevertheless, the Sorbonne found the *Tiers Livre* stuffed with heresy, and condemned it; Rabelais was obliged to seek refuge at Metz. At that time, the Sorbonne would have found heresy in anything which Rabelais wrote, since the years 1545-6 mark a period of violent reaction against the Humanists and the Réformés. In 1547, the great patron of the arts, King François 1er, died, and du Bellay was sent to Rome. He took Rabelais with him, stopping in Lyon on the way long enough for the author to hand in the first eleven chapters of the *Quart Livre*, which appeared in 1549. They were preceded by a long prologue in which Rabelais for the first time allowed himself a desperate cry of anguish and anger against the powers which had vilified him for so long, and made his statement on the iniquitous and dangerous use of censorship:

> Si par ces termes entendez les calumniateurs de mes escripts, plus aptement les pourrez nommer diables. Car, en grec, calumnie est dicte diabole . . . Je les nomme

diables noirs, blancs, diables privez, diables domesticques. Et ce que ont faict envers mes livres, ilz feront (si on les laisse faire) envers tous aultres.

Rabelais's new protector, Cardinal Odet de Châtillon, encouraged him nevertheless to finish the book, which finally appeared in 1552 with a letter of dedication to Châtillon in which the anger, slightly less violent, was reiterated:

> Mais la calumnie de certains Canibales, misantropes, agelastes, avoit tant contre moi esté atroce et desraisonnée qu'elle avoit vaincu ma patience et plus n'estois délibéré en escrire un iota. Car l'une des moindres contumelies dont ilz usoient estoit que telz livres tous estoient farciz d'heresies diverses. . . . d'heresies poinct, sinon perversement et contre tout usaige de raison et de languaige commun . . . si en ma vie, escriptz, parolles, voire certes pensées, je recognoissois scintille aulcune heresie . . . par moymesmes à l'example du Phoenix, seroit le bois sec amassé, et le feu allumé, pour en icelluy me brusler.

But I was so hideously and baselessly slandered by certain cannibals, misanthropists, and sour-pusses that I lost all patience and decided not to write another word. One of the lesser accusations that they made against me was that my books were crammed full of different heresies. . . . But heresies are there none, except for those who make perverse interpretations and twist plain statements and common speech . . . if I detected any spark of heresy in my life, my writings, my words, or even in my thoughts . . . I would myself imitate the Phoenix, pile up the dry wood, light the fire, and burn myself to death.

The *Quart Livre,* like the *Tiers Livre,* is topical. Since the discovery of Canada by Jacques Cartier in 1524, tales of voyages of discovery had become increasingly popular. Rabelais therefore devotes his fourth book to the narration of Pantagruel's and Panurge's quest for the Divine Bottle, which will eventually solve the question of Panurge's marriage. The nautical details of the voyage are astonishingly accurate, particularly in the famous bravura storm scene. The various ports of call which the travellers make enable Rabelais to resume his satirical vein. One especially violent episode describes the inhabitants of the 'isle de Papimanes', and is an overt mockery of the Vatican. When the book was written, relations between the new king, Henri II, and the Pope were not happy, so that Rabelais was on fairly safe ground in attacking the Papal Court; he may even have done so with royal connivance. However, by the time the book was published, the quarrel between Paris and the Vatican had been patched up, with the inevitable result that the *Quart Livre* was condemned by the Sorbonne and by order of Parliament. Rabelais, by now curate of Meudon, disappears from view. There is an unattested story that he was imprisoned in Lyon. He died in Paris in April 1553. Nine years later there appeared a sequel to the *Quart Livre* called *l'Isle Sonante*, and in 1564 the *Cinquiesme Livre* (including the sixteen chapters of *l'Isle Sonante*) which may or may not have been partly written by Rabelais; the matter is still disputed.

As far as is known, François Rabelais never married. He is variously estimated to have fathered between one and three children, all of whom died in infancy.

2
The Renaissance in France

At the beginning of the sixteenth century, at least nine out of ten Frenchmen were illiterate. The few that could claim to be educated learned mathematics, rhetoric, logic, astronomy; it was not considered that the study of literature had anything to do with education or could possibly make a valid contribution to the shaping of a young mind. Some Latin writers were known, but were not studied in the modern sense of the word, for their own intrinsic value; they were on the syllabus because they supported pre-conceived notions, or rather because they could be made to appear to support such notions. Virgil, for example, had announced the birth of Jesus (!) and so was revered as a prophet; but he was also considered a magician. Ovid's works were equally full of Christian revelations. The only Greek writer of significance was Aristotle, whose every pronouncement was accepted as a revelation of the truth; indeed, Aristotle was a pillar of the Church! The critical faculty was entirely absent. Knowledge was the prerogative of the Church, whose influence was felt in every sphere of life. It was hardly possible to live and breathe without the sanction of the Church, whose authority governed every social, economic and intellectual activity from the cradle to the grave. Latin was the language of the scholars, but it was a very poor Latin, vulgarized almost beyond the point of recognition and heavily influenced by jargon and local syntax. There were as yet no dictionaries, so that anyone who wished to learn had to do so through the medium of this coarse, artificial Latin and within the rigid framework of medieval scholastic traditions, the scope of which was severely limited.

The wars with Italy revealed to the French a country which might have been on another planet. They discovered flourishing cities and palaces, a new class of 'bourgeois' made wealthy by the rise of Capitalism, and above all a feverish intellectual activity. The Italian Renaissance had been well under way for some time, and exciting discoveries and experiments had been made in all branches of the arts and sciences. In particular, the Italians had seen Latin literature with entirely fresh eyes. Not content with medieval commentaries on the old texts, they had gone to the texts themselves to find out what they really said. This desire had in turn led to the systematic search for forgotten manuscripts. Petrarch found a manuscript of Cicero's correspondence. Boccacio found some manuscripts of Tacitus, Poggio found Lucretius' *De Rerum Natura*. The discovery of texts such as these had re-established Classical Latin as a language of literary value for the clear expression of ideas, far above the vulgar philological anachronism of Medieval Latin. It seemed that literature was being reborn. The Italians went even further in their joyful search. They rediscovered Greek literature, which had lain in oblivion for ten centuries. Latin literature was revealed to be a literature of imitation; the Greeks had said and thought it all before the Romans! Hellenic studies, and particularly the study of Plato, became a factor of cardinal importance in the Renaissance. New ideas (or rather old ideas re-discovered) were welcomed with a monumental thirst for knowledge, all knowledge and any knowledge, which one might aptly call Gargantuan. The first courses in Greek were established in Florence.

One can imagine with what fervour the French returned to their homeland, and how ardently they set about reading forgotten texts for themselves. The French Renaissance has been rightly called a period of revolution and upheaval, but it was a revolution only in so far as it was characterized by a fierce denial of the immediate past, a fervent wish to escape from the rigid and unthinking dogmas of medieval learning.

Although the French Renaissance sprang originally from the Italian, it differed from the latter in two important aspects:

1. The Italians had matured since their first period of greedy accumulation of all knowledge, and had evolved a sense of Beauty, of Art, which was as much concerned with Form as with Content. The French Humanists of 1530–50, when Rabelais was writing, had not reached this stage. With few exceptions, they were still eagerly gathering knowledge with scant regard for the way in which their thoughts were expressed. One had to wait for Ronsard and du Bellay for a keen appreciation of Form.

2. While the Italians devoted their energies to seeing pagan literature in a new perspective, the Northern Europeans who followed them, including the French, carried the critical approach one step further and applied it to Christian texts. By examining many sacred texts in the original Greek, they discovered that some hallowed Christian dogmas were founded on poor evidence. Such an objective treatment of sacred literature inevitably aroused the hostility of the Church, whose authority it challenged and indeed threatened. It was suggested that the Church had lost sight of the original teachings of the apostles, had forgotten their purity of spirit, and had sunk into such corruption that it no longer earned the respect of thoughtful people. Medieval religious practices were first questioned, then condemned, and were finally thought to be in serious need of reform. Thus was born the Reform, largely misunderstood and misinterpreted by the Church, which could brook no criticism of its word, and this in turn engendered the religious wars of the second half of the sixteenth century.

We are now in a position to examine exactly what the word 'Humanism' meant to Frenchmen in 1530, the year when François 1er founded the College of France and Rabelais was taking his medical degree in Montpellier. Humanism has come to be a label covering a very wide range of views, connected only by their primary concern with Man, his value, his potentialities, his significance. In 1530 the word has a narrower application. Derived from *Humanitas*, it meant the pursuit of culture and science for their own sake, the conquest of knowledge as an end in itself.

These, then, are the principal traits of French Humanism:

1. The Discovery of Antiquity

Weary of the stultified medieval commentaries on the texts of antiquity, the French Humanists follow the Italians in their study of original manuscripts. They seek to understand the old texts in all their purity, to explain them, to translate them afresh, and to make them available more widely than before. In this, the role of the printing press is an important one. With the invention of printing, books are no longer the hidden manuscripts known only to a handful of men, but objects which many people can possess, read, and digest. Without the printing press, Humanism may well have passed unnoticed, the intellectual amusement of a small club.

The Humanists approached the texts of antiquity with a new *critical spirit*. The intoxication of discovering such a wealth of forgotten knowledge meant that they had almost to relearn how to read. In order to assist them in this task, and to assist other Frenchmen to whom they wished their knowledge to spread by means of their new critical translations, they had to create the instruments of understanding – books of grammar and dictionaries. The first dictionaries of the Latin language were written at this time, usually the superhuman effort of one man. It was in this domain of philology that the French Humanists really came into their own. Robert Estienne published his *Thesaurus Linguae Latinae* in 1535, Henri Estienne a *Thesaurus Linguae Graecae* in 1572, Etienne Dolet a *Commentarii Linguae Latinae* between 1536 and 1538. The first intelligent translations into French were also given, translations which were no longer simple paraphrases. Calvin published a French version of his important *Institution Chrétienne* five years after the Latin version in 1535. Amyot translated Plutarch. Marot published a version of the *Psalms* in French verse. Furthermore, Budé was the first to study Roman Law by going directly to the texts, and also the first to propose a theory of education in which the study of ancient literature (there was as yet no 'modern' literature) played a necessary role in a man's intellectual formation.

Although medieval scholars had had some knowledge of Latin texts, and of a few Greek texts in Latin translation, they had used them to support Christian doctrines. The Humanists sought to read ancient texts for their intrinsic value, independent of their possible theological application. The pagan life which they revealed was admired for itself, and was not thought necessarily to be relevant to religious thought.

2. The Analysis of Sacred Texts

Humanism in Italy had been essentially pagan and aesthetic. In Germany, England, and especially France, however, the Humanist thinkers were very much concerned with religious and moral questions. They applied the same spirit of informed criticism to their reading of the Bible as they did to Latin and Greek writers. The Church had actually discouraged its followers from reading the Bible at all; it preferred to disseminate only its own version of the Scriptures, its own selections and interpretations. The Humanists would have none of this. They went to the original Greek text of the New Testament, analysed it, translated it, made it freely available to everyone. The great Erasmus, whom all the Humanists admired and revered, was the first to publish the Greek text, Lefèvre d'Étaples the first to publish a French translation. People then rose in anger against the immense temporal authority of the Pope, his riches, his political ambitions, none of which they found justified in the Scriptures. Once it was realized that the Church could and should be opposed in certain areas, a small minority of Humanists advocated something approaching atheism. Such was the case with Bonaventure des Périers and Étienne Dolet, for example. But they are exceptional. For the most part, it did not seem contradictory to be Humanist *and* Christian, and most of the attacks against the Church were inspired by religious fervour. The Humanists sought merely to re-establish revealed truth, hidden beneath a multiplicity of meaningless rites and base corruptions.

3. The Scientific Spirit

Little progress had been made in the sciences in Europe for almost ten centuries. With the discovery of Greece, a whole new world of scientific advance was revealed. The Greeks had known and evolved everything – Geometry, Mathematics, Architecture, Engineering, Astronomy; most were in fact Greek words, Greek inventions. Rabelais was one of the first to read Greek medical works in the original. The rediscovery of science had been initiated in Italy, by such men as Copernicus (Polish, but living in Italy), Giordano Bruno, Galileo Galilei, Leonardo da Vinci. The French Humanists, in their wild eagerness to plumb the depths of all branches of knowledge, embraced this new spirit with enthusiasm. One finds many a reference to scientific knowledge in the works of Rabelais, who had obviously read everything he could lay his hands on. It would be wrong, however, to regard this frantic gathering of scientific data as contributing in any way to a diminution of religious feeling. That result came much later. The theory of Copernicus, that the earth revolved around the sun, did not explode like a bomb in France. This, and other theories, were examined with eager intellectual curiosity without troubling religious beliefs. The upheaval of accepted dogmas was indeed the ultimate effect, but it was slow to make itself felt, and plays but a small part in the intellectual climate of France in 1530.

4. Confidence in Human Nature

The discovery of the Greeks revealed what a vast culture the human mind could conceive and achieve, of what great things men were capable. Why should they not be capable of such achievements again, and why should not men progress even further along the road of cultural advance? The Universal Man, who knew no limits to his endeavours, became an object of veneration. In Italy, Raphael, Cellini, Pico della Mirandola, and especially Leonardo da Vinci were admired. Leonardo, who was sage, artist, poet, sculptor, engineer, physician, architect, musician, mathematician, and much more besides, was the ideal of the complete man with encyclopedic knowledge. By emulating men such as these, the French Humanists implied that men must not stop in their search for truth, that they must not be complacent, that they can, and should, advance towards the Utopia of Thomas More. 'L'humanisme est une éthique de confiance en la nature humaine', writes A. Renaudet,[1] 'il commande à l'homme un effort constant pour réaliser en lui le type idéal de l'homme, à la société un effort constant pour réaliser la perfection des rapports humains. Ainsi conçu, il exige un immense effort de culture'. Being difficult to reconcile with the dogma of Original Sin and with traditional pessimism of Medieval Christianity, this confidence in human nature was eventually to contribute to the spirit of Reform.

5. The Sense of Beauty

Humanists read the ancient texts not in order to confirm preconceived ideas, nor even only to taste and savour the new ideas which they contained. They developed in time a keen

[1] *Humanisme*, in *Dictionnaire des Lettres Françaises*.

appreciation of the beauty of literature, of the value of form, concision, economy, the shape and structure of a piece of prose. This aspect of Humanism, in which erudition gives way to *le goût*, and the gluttony of knowledge accumulated is replaced by the growth of literature, had already developed in Italy in the fifteenth century. In France, there were small signs of such taste in 1530, and precious little indication of it in the works of Rabelais. Medieval disorder persisted well into the sixteenth century, bringing with it a total absence of any sense of harmony or proportion. The author spoke with a wide variety of voices, mingling broad humour with mysticism and serious discussion, sometimes on the same page or even within the same sentence.

These, then, are the main characteristics of the Renaissance in France in 1530. All find their echo in the works of François Rabelais, with the exception of the last. When Rabelais tells us in his Prologue to *Gargantua* that his book is not as silly as it might seem:

> les matières icy traictées ne sont tant folastres comme le titre au-dessus prétendoit
>
> The subjects here treated are not so foolish as the title on the cover suggested

and exhorts us not to be put off by the apparently frivolous nature of story (l'habit ne faict poinct le moyne) but to

> soigneusement peser ce que y est déduict
>
> carefully weigh up the contents of this book

he is warning us that the narrative contains some pertinent discussions which he wants us to take seriously. These discussions will centre on themes dear to the Humanists – morals,

THE RENAISSANCE IN FRANCE 21

education, politics, the Church – and will contain much acute observation of French society. Rabelais wants his readers to

> par curieuse leçon et méditation fréquente, rompre l'os et sugcer la sustantificque moelle.
>
> by diligent reading and frequent meditation, you must break the bone and lick out the substantial marrow.

Émile Faguet and Jean Plattard both claim that Rabelais is gently pulling our leg in this Prologue, that he is suggesting that we should be just as foolish to seek a 'message' in his writings as the medieval scholars had been to find a body of Christian doctrine in Ovid. But this mockery of the reader is simply part of the curious mixture of tone which characterizes the whole book, a mixture of humour, pedantry, and Humanist propaganda. It is clear that, although the giants accomplish feats of prodigious absurdity which produce a comic effect, they are guided by ethics of conduct which Rabelais invites us to follow. Furthermore, his satires betray a partisan spirit which indicate a desire to teach as much as to observe. His picture of French society is not entirely objective; he ridicules certain customs, condemns others. In other words, he not only describes what he sees, he also passes judgement. As Pierre Jourda has written:

> Rabelais inaugure la lignée des écrivains pour qui la peinture du vrai est un moyen d'amélioration morale.
> (*Le Gargantua de Rabelais*, p. 90)

We must now therefore taste the substance and marrow of Rabelais's books, and see in what ways he represents the Renaissance in France. He belongs to the Renaissance
1. by his Humanism, his absolute confidence in ancient culture;
2. by his style, often an imitation of the best Ciceronian prose; *also medieval genre.*

3. by his Naturalism, or more precisely optimism, confidence in the ultimate good of human nature, and its possibilities as a civilizing influence;
4. by his rejection of the immediate past, the dark corridors of the Middle Ages. It is a fundamental and recurring theme with Rabelais that men have emerged from an age of darkness into a new age of enlightenment. He has nothing but contempt for all that is medieval, the Sorbonne, the monks.

3
The Humanism of Rabelais

A. La Restitution Des Bonnes Lettres

When, in 1530, François 1er founded the collège des lecteurs royaux (later to become the Collège de France), dedicated to the teaching of Latin, Greek and Hebrew, and independent of the authority of the Sorbonne, it was a moment of triumph for the Humanists. Rabelais, writing in 1532, was one of the first to celebrate the event, with a magnificent piece of prose, justly famous, which amounts to a Humanist *profession de foi*. It is a letter which Gargantua writes to his son Pantagruel while the latter is studying in Paris:

> Maintenant toutes disciplines sont restituées, les langues instaurées: grecque, sans laquelle c'est honte que une personne se die sçavant, hébraïcque, caldaïcque, latine;
> ... Tout le monde est plein de gens savans, de précepteurs très doctes, de libraires très amples, et m'est advis que, ny au temps de Platon, ny de Cicéron, ny de Papinian, n'estoit telle commodité d'estude qu'on y veoit maintenant.
> ... le temps n'estoit tant idoine ne commode ès lettres comme est de présent, et n'avoys copie de telz précepteurs comme tu as eu. Le temps estoit encores ténébreux et sentant l'infélicité et calamité des Gothz, qui avoient mis à destruction toute bonne litérature. Mais, par la bonté divine, la lumière et dignité a esté de mon eage rendue ès lettres. . . .
> ... Par quoy, mon filz, je te admoneste que employe ta jeunesse à bien profiter en estudes et en vertus. . . .
> (*Pantagruel*, VIII)

> Now every method of teaching has been restored, and the study of languages has been revived: of Greek, without which it is disgraceful for a man to call himself a scholar, and of Hebrew, Chaldean, and Latin.... The whole world is full of learned men, of very erudite tutors, and of most extensive libraries, and it is my opinion that neither in the time of Plato, of Cicero, nor of Papinian were there such facilities for study as one finds today ... the times were not as fit and favourable for learning as they are today, and I had no supply of tutors such as you have. Indeed the times were still dark, and mankind was perpetually reminded of the miseries and disasters wrought by those Goths who had destroyed all sound scholarship. But, thanks be to God, learning has been restored in my age to its former dignity and enlightenment.... Therefore, my son, I beg you to devote your youth to the firm pursuit of your studies and to the attainment of virtue.

The whole of this letter should be read for the picture it gives of the intellectual climate prevalent among Humanists in 1532. Two years later, 'après la restitution des bonnes lettres' (*Gargantua*, IX), the enthusiasm has not abated:

> quelle différence y a entre le sçavoir de voz resveurs matéologiens du temps jadis et les jeunes gens de maintenant. (*Gargantua*, XV)

> What difference there is between the knowledge of your old-time nonsensological babblers and the young people of today.

Throughout the work of Rabelais, the same high note of confidence persists, the same contempt for the Dark Ages is maintained. At the very end of the Fifth Book, when the travellers finally encounter the Divine Bottle and seek its advice, this is given in one word, *Trinch*! Drink what? Drink wine, yes, because 'en vin est vérité cachée' (*Cinquième Livre*, XLV), but more than this, drink as much learning, knowledge and wisdom as you are able, for there is still much to learn. The ancient sages may point the way, but 'tout le sçavoir et d'eulx et de leurs prédécesseurs à peine estre la minime partie de ce qui est, et ne le sçavent'. (*Cinquième Livre*, XLVII)

> All men's knowledge, both theirs and their forefathers', is hardly an infinitesimal fraction of all that exists and that they do not know.

There is ample evidence that Rabelais's own reading has been monumental in its scope. There is scarcely a writer or a poet whose works he has not read and devoured, to which he does not make reference when relevance permits. The list is so huge that it is not practicable to enumerate the writers whom Rabelais mentions. One should, however, note his homage to Socrates in the Prologue to *Gargantua*:

> entendement plus que humain, vertus merveilleuse, couraige invincible, sobresse non pareille, contentement certain, asseurance parfaicte, déprisement incroyable de tout ce pourquoy les humains tant veiglent, courent, travaillent, navigent, et bataillent.

> A superhuman understanding, miraculous virtue, invincible courage, unrivalled sobriety, unfailing contentment, perfect confidence, and an incredible contempt for all those things men so watch for, pursue, work for, sail after, and struggle for.

There are also many examples of Rabelais's admiration for contemporary Humanists, particular among which is the letter to Erasmus already quoted in the Biographical Introduction to this book. We have also a letter written to Jean du Bellay, in which Rabelais thanks his protector for having taken him to Rome, 'capitale du monde', and praises du Bellay for being 'l'homme le plus docte qui soit sous le ciel, et le plus humain'. Another object of Rabelais's admiration was Lefèvre d'Étaples, translator of the Bible into French. Abel Lefranc is of the opinion that the theologian Hippothadée, in the *Tiers Livre*, is based on Lefèvre d'Étaples and is a testimony of Rabelais's veneration of the great Humanist. Certainly, Hippothadée is the only theologian for whom Rabelais has a good word.

Humanists were concerned not only with reading as many of the Latin and Greek writers as they could, but also with emulating their style. Gargantua advises Pantagruel, in the famous letter, to bear this in mind:

> et que tu formes ton style quant à la grecque, à l'imitation de Platon, quant à la latine, à Cicéron.
>
> (*Pantagruel*, VIII)

Rabelais's own style, in his more serious chapters, is patently inspired by the fine periodic sentences of the best Latin prose. The letter to Erasmus, Gargantua's letter to Pantagruel, the reference to Socrates in the Prologue to *Gargantua*, Gargantua's speech on marriage (*Tiers Livre*, XLVIII), his address to the vanquished enemy at the end of the Picrocholine War (*Gargantua*, L), all are splendid examples of elaborate Ciceronian style.

B. La Sorbonne

Hand in hand with a celebration of the Renaissance goes a scornful disdain for those who resist it, notably the Sorbonne. Rabelais ridicules the complacency of medieval scholars, their stubborn refusal to be enlightened, the atrocious bastardized Latin which they use in their universities, and the useless sophistry of their specious argumentation.

1. *Janotus*

Gargantua has stolen the bells from Notre-Dame de Paris. (*Gargantua*, XVII). In order to recover them, the Sorbonne sends a deputy to remonstrate with Gargantua, one Janotus de Bragmardo. The scholar begins his speech by saying all that needs to be said, a simple and direct request for the return of the bells:

> Ce ne seroyt que bon que nous rendissiez nos cloches, car elles nous font bien besoing. (*Gargantua*, XIX)

It would only be right if you were to give us back our bells, for we are greatly in need of them.

Not content with this, however, he proceeds to elaborate on the theme in a mixture of French and appallingly bad Latin:

> Or sus, *de parte Dei, date nobis clochas nostras*. . . . O Monsieur, *Domine, clochidonnaminor nobis!* Dea, *est bonum urbis*. Tout le monde s'en sert. Si votre jument s'en trouve bien, aussi faict nostre Faculté . . . Ça, je vous prouve que me les doibvez bailler. *Ego sic argumentor: Omnis clocha clochabilis, in clocherio clochando*, etc.
> (*Gargantua*, XIX)

> Well now, in God's name, give us back our bells. O sir, *Domine clochidonnaminor nobis*. Indeed, they are the property of the city. Everybody uses them. If they suit your mare, they also suit our Faculty. See now, I prove to you that you ought to give them to me. This is how I argue. [The rest is untranslatable.]

Rabelais was justifiably horrified by the improper and ungrammatical use of a language which could be so lucid and precise. In the glossary which he appended to his *Quart Livre* many years later, he defined 'Solecisme' as 'vicieuse manière de parler.' Janotus personifies all that is wrong with medieval scholasticism. Krailsheimer has aptly called him a 'pedantic fossil'.

2. *L'Écolier Limousin*

While Rabelais castigates Janotus for murdering Classical Latin, he is equally harsh towards the Limousin student who latinizes the French language. Pantagruel meets this student one day in Paris, and asks him where he comes from. The reply is scarcely comprehensible:

> De l'alme, inclyte et célèbre académie que l'on vocite Lutèce.
> (*Pantagruel*, VI)

Having at length understood that the man means he is from Paris, Pantagruel questions him further and asks how he spends his time there.

> Nous transfretons la Sequane au dilucule et crépuscule; nous déambulons par les compites et quadrivies de l'urbe; nous despumons la verbocination latiale, etc., etc.
>
> (Ibid.)

'What devil of a language is this?' exclaims Pantagruel, 'Qu'est-ce que veult dire ce fol?' One of his friends explains that the student is trying to mimic fashionable Parisian speech, but succeeds only in murdering Latin:

> il ne fait que escorcher le latin et cuide ainsi pindariser, et luy semble bien qu'il est quelque grand orateur en françoys, parce qu'il dédaigne l'usance commun de parler.
>
> (Ibid.)

All he is doing is murdering Latin. He thinks he is pindarizing, and imagines he's a great orator in French because he disdains the common use of speech.

The satire on Janotus is doubtless a caricature,[1] but the language used by the 'écolier limousin' is hardly exaggerated. All courses at the university were given in Latin, it being the only language of scholarship. The students were given to using obscure Latinisms in their everyday speech, from a kind of academic snobbery. Rabelais, a philological purist like all Humanists of his time, detests such pretentious nonsense and dismisses the hybrid language as gibberish. Pantagruel's parting words to the Limousin, when the latter finally reverts to his native tongue on being threatened with violence, are:

> A ceste heure parle-tu naturellement.   (Ibid.)

[1] Although, according to Pierre Villey (*Marot et Rabelais*), it is based on fact.

3. *Saint-Victor*

Rabelais gives a joyously irreverent catalogue of the books on the shelves at the Librairie de Saint-Victor (*Pantagruel* VII), visited by Pantagruel in Paris. It contains such titles as *The Codpiece of the Law, The Elephantine Testicle of the Valiant, The Prelates' Bagpipe,* and hosts of others. Saint-Victor is a satire on the scholarly works then available, packed full of useless information and endless argumentation over nothing. They are the books of the sophists.

4. *Blanc et Bleu*

In Chapters IX and X of *Gargantua*, Rabelais gives a long and reasoned explanation of the significance of white and blue, being the colours worn by Gargantua. According to tradition, he says, white stood for faith and blue for steadfastness, but this tradition was dictated by:

> des tyrans qui voulent leur arbitre tenir lieu de raison, non des saiges et sçavans qui par raisons manifestes contentent les lecteurs. (*Gargantua*, IX)

> Tyrants who would have their will take the place of reason, not the wise and learned, who satisfy their readers with display of evidence.

As Janotus also says:

> Raison, nous n'en usons poinct céans. (*Gargantua*, XX)

> Reason, we use none of that here!

Rabelais shows that he is quite as adept at proving night to be day, and shows, by inductive logic, that white stands for joy and blue for Heavenly things. He is here mocking the ability of the Sorbonne sophists to devote their energies to interminable arguments over trivia, from which one learns nothing. He is just as disdainful of their style in so doing:

stille de ramonneur de cheminée ou de cuisinier et marmiteux. (*Pantagruel*, X)

The style of a chimney-sweep, or a cook, or a scullion.

5. *Propos Torcheculatif*

By far the funniest satire on the sophists is the chapter wherein Gargantua shows his 'marvellous intelligence, by his invention of an Arse-wipe'. With one absurd syllogism piled upon another, the youthful giant expounds his 'propos torcheculatif' with joyful obscenity:

Il n'est (dist Gargantua) poinct besoing torcher cul, sinon qu'il y ayt ordure; ordure n'y peut estre si on n'a chié; chier donc nous fault davant que le cul torcher.
(*Gargantua*, XIII)

There's no need to wipe your bottom unless it's mucky, said Gargantua, it can't be mucky if you haven't shat; we have to shit, therefore, before we wipe our arses.

and he concludes:

je dys et maintiens qu'il n'y a tel torchecul que d'un oyzon bien dumeté, pourveu qu'on luy tienne la teste entre les jambes. Et m'en croyez sus mon honneur. Car vous sentez au trou du cul une volupté mirificque, tant par la doulceur d'icelluy dumet que par la chaleur tempérée de l'oizon. . . . Et ne pensez que la béatitude des héroes et semi dieux, qui sont par les Champs Elysiens, soit en leur asphodèle, ou ambroise, ou nectar, comme disent ces vieilles ycy. Elle est (scelon mon opinion) en ce qu'ilz se torchent le cul d'un oyzon, et telle est l'opinion de Maistre Jehan d'Escosse. (*Ibid.*)

I say and maintain that there is no arse-wiper like a well-downed goose, if you hold her neck between your legs. You must take my word for it, you really must. You get a miraculous sensation in your arse-hole, both from the softness of the down and from the temperate heat of the goose herself. . . . Do not imagine that the felicity of the heroes and demigods in the Elysian Fields arises from their asphodel, their ambrosia, or their nectar, as those ancients say. It comes, in my opinion, from their wiping their arses with the neck of a goose, and that is the opinion of Master Duns Scotus too.

6. *Par Signe*

Another very vivid satire on sophistry is contained in the chapter in which Panurge encounters an Englishman (Thaumaste) who, disdaining to speak, conducts a conversation in sign language (*Pantagruel*, XIX). The signs which he uses to score a point are elaborately absurd and convey nothing; they serve only to show the man up as a clown. Rabelais intends his readers to reflect upon the parallel that exists between these nonsensical gestures and the purely mechanical arguments of the sophists; both, he implies, spend a great deal of time getting nowhere.

7. *L'Apologie des Dettes*

The first few chapters of the *Tiers Livre* are devoted to Panurge's defence of his indebtedness. Penniless, Panurge sets about persuading Pantagruel to pay his debts on his behalf. He embarks on a lengthy discourse in praise of lenders and borrowers which recalls the spurious and convoluted argumentation employed by the sophists. Pantagruel is not convinced, but pays up nevertheless.

4
On Education

A. L'Ancienne Pédagogie

Rabelais's contempt for the Sorbonne is not confined to its influence upon university life. The influence was felt at all levels of education, and Rabelais paints a finely detailed picture of the kind of education which obtained during his own youth. He describes how the giant Grandgousier engaged a certain Maîstre Thubal Holoferne (a fictitious name derived from Biblical references) to be tutor to his son Gargantua, the methods used by this tutor, and their results. First of all, Holoferne teaches his pupil to learn the alphabet by heart:

> luy aprint sa charte si bien qu'il la disoit par cueur au rebours; et y fut cinq ans et troys mois. Puis luy leut *Donat*, le *Facet*, *Theodolet* et Alanus *in Parabolis*; et y fut treze ans six moys et deux sepmaines.
>
> (*Gargantua*, XIV)

> taught him his letters so well that he said them by heart backwards; and he took five years and three months to do that; then the sophist read to him Donatus [a Medieval Latin Grammar], Facetus [on Civil Law], Theodolus [a mythological Treatise], and Alanus *in Parabolis* [Moral Precepts], which took thirteen years six months and a fortnight.

Gargantua 'aprenoit à escripre gotticquement, (he learnt how to write the Gothic script) and used the stock medieval grammar *De Modis Significandi*, which he also was required to commit to memory:

Et le sceut si bien que, au coupelaud, il le rendait par cueur à revers, et prouvait sus ses doigtz à sa mère que *de modis significandi non erat scientia.*

And Gargantua knew the book so well that at testing-time he repeated it backwards by heart, proving to his mother on his fingers that Grammar was no science. [Using his fingers to enumerate in sequence the syllogistic points.]

Various other standard medieval texts were stuffed down the throat of the poor Gargantua, as a result of which, Rabelais tells us, he became as wise as any man baked in an oven.

Rabelais here rejects with considerable scorn the medieval practice of forcing the child to commit to memory a stack of useless information and syllogistic methods of reasoning. The effect of such methods is not to educate the child, says Rabelais, but only to fill his mind with meaningless notions:

mieulz luy vauldroit rien n'aprendre que telz libres soubz telz précepteurs aprendre, car leur sçavoir n'estoit que besterie et leur sapience n'estoit que moufles, abastardisant les bons et nobles esperitz et corrompent toute fleur de jeunesse.

(*Gargantua,* XV)

it was better for the boy to learn nothing than to study such books under such masters. For their learning was mere stupidity, and their wisdom like an empty glove; it bastardized good and noble minds and corrupted all the flower of youth.

Furthermore, Gargantua's bodily health had been neglected as much as his mental well-being. He arose late in the day (between eight and nine in the morning), stretched himself and lay in bed for some time 'the better to rouse his animal spirits', and dressed in abominable fashion. He combed his hair with four fingers and a thumb:

car ses précepteurs disoient que soy aultrement pigner, laver et nettoyer estoit perdre temps en ce monde.

(*Gargantua*, XXI)

For his tutors said that to comb or wash or clean oneself in any other way was to lose time in this world.

B. La Nouvelle Pédagogie

In opposition to the old methods, which had succeeded in making Gargantua simple, ignorant, and stupid, Rabelais proposes a programme of study which is a perfect expression of the hope and confidence inherent in Humanist culture. Grandgousier appoints a new tutor, Ponocrates, under whose guidance the infant Gargantua gradually strengthens in mind and body. The methods employed anticipate, in many respects, educationalists of a much later date. The salient principles of the programme are:

1. That no time should be wasted, every precious minute of Gargantua's day (which starts at 4.00 a.m.) must be usefully employed. There is no place for lethargy. Even mealtimes are used for revision and intelligent discussion.

il ne perdoit heure quelconques du jour, ains tout son temps consommoit en lettres et honeste sçavoir.

(*Gargantua*, XXIII)

he did not waste an hour of the day, but spent his entire time on literature and sound learning.

2. Certain times can be set aside for games and relaxation but both must be instructive rather than escapist and must be freely embraced rather than imposed. Conversely, tedious studies can be made a pleasure if the tutor turns them into an interesting amusement. In this way, Gargantua learns his tables

ON EDUCATION

> pour y aprendre mille petites gentillesses et inventions nouvelles, lesquelles toutes yssoient de arithmétique.

so that he might learn a thousand little tricks and new inventions, all based on arithmetic.

> En ce moyen entra en affection de icelle science numérale.
> (Ibid.)

In this way he came to love this science of numbers.

Rousseau, Locke and Fénelon were all to echo these precepts; Fénelon wrote that the tutor should learn how to 'mêler l'instruction avec le jeu'.

3. *Physical education* is just as essential as intellectual education. Rabelais's medical training is brought into play at this point. The body must be kept healthy so that the mind may profit. Hygiene is of paramount importance as are physical exercises and recreational activities which are not merely cerebral – horse-riding, dancing, swimming, fencing, running, etc. The purpose is not only to keep the mind clear, but to develop a virility which may one day be called upon in time of war. Moreover, the pupil's diet must be carefully planned.

4. *The tutor must place himself on a level with the student*, pretend to be ignorant and give the impression that he is learning with his charge. A sympathy and companionship may then arise between teacher and pupil, and education made to be a shared activity. As Rousseau was later to write, in *Émile*, 'Qu'il croie toujours être le maître, et que ce soit toujours vous qui le soyez.'

5. *The scope of Gargantua's studies must be encyclopedic.* A Humanist training encompasses every branch of learning – geometry, music, astronomy, botany, and so on. When

Gargantua has grown into an adult, he passes on to his son Pantagruel the same advice (*Pantagruel*, VIII), but in greater detail. Pantagruel is to read philology, philosophy, astronomy (but not astrology, which he must avoid, it being guesswork rather than learning), law, ornithology, botany, mineralogy, medicine, etc. The aim here is obviously to become a 'uomo universale' like Leonardo da Vinci.

6. The scientific elements of this programme are to be practically applied. It is not sufficient to read botany and astronomy: one's reading must be followed by what we should now call field work – collecting plants and examing them, observing the stars, and becoming proficient in the necessary techniques.

7. All the bookwork must refer to the original texts, not to translations or 'working texts'.

8. La Divine Escripture is a text to be read aloud. The day finishes with prayers of thanks to God,

> le glorifiant de sa bonté immense, et, luy rendant grâce de tout le temps passé, se recommandoient à sa divine clémence pour tout l'advenir. (Ibid.)

> glorifying Him for His immense goodness, rendering thanks to Him for all the past, and recommending themselves to His divine clemency for all the future.

These, then, are the broad outlines of the Humanist programme; for the details, Rabelais needs no commentary:

> Se esveilloit doncques Gargantua environ quatre heures du matin. Cependant qu'on le frotoit, luy estoit leue quelque pagine de la divine Escripture haultement et clerement, avec pronunciation competente à la matière. . . . Puis alloit ès lieux secretz faire excretion des digestions naturelles. Là son précepteur répétoit ce que avoit esté leu, luy

exposant les poinctz plus obscurs et difficiles. Eux retornans, consideroient l'estat du ciel: si tel estoit comme l'avoient noté au soir précédent, et quelz signes entroit le soleil, aussi la lune, pour icelle journée. Ce faict, estoit habillé, peigné, testonné, accoustré et parfumé, durant lequel temps on luy répétoit les leçons du jour d'avant. . . . Puis par trois bonnes heures luy estoit faicte lecture. Ce faict, yssoient hors, tousjours conférens des propoz de la lecture, et se desportoient en Bracque ou es préz, et jouoient à la balle, à la paulme, à la pile trigone, *galentement se exercens les corps comme ilz avoient les âmes auparavant exercé*.[1] Tout leur jeu n'estoit qu'en liberté, car ilz laissoient la partie quand leur plaisoit et cessoient ordinairement lors que suoient parmy le corps, ou estoient aultrement las. Adoncq estoient très bien essuéz et frottéz, changeoient de chemise et, doulcement se pourmenans, alloient veoir sy le disner estoit prest. (Ibid.)

Gargantua now woke about four o'clock in the morning and, whilst he was being rubbed down, had some chapter of Holy Writ read to him loudly and clearly, with a pronunciation befitting the matter. . . . Then he went into some private place to make excretion of his natural waste-products, and there his tutor repeated what had been read, explaining to him the more obscure and difficult points. On their way back, they considered the face of the sky, whether it was as they had observed it the night before, and into what sign the sun, and also the moon, were entering for that day. This done, Gargantua was dressed, combed, curled, trimmed and perfumed, and meanwhile the previous day's lessons were repeated to him. . . . Then for three full hours he was read to. When this was done, they went out, still discussing the subjects of the reading, and walked over to the sign of the Hound or to the Meadows, where they played ball or tennis or the triangle game, gaily exercising their bodies as they had previously exercised their minds. Their sports were entirely unconstrained. For they gave up the game whenever they pleased, and usually stopped when their whole bodies were sweating, or when they were otherwise tired. Then they were well dried and rubbed down, changed their shirts, and sauntered off to see if dinner was ready.

[1] My italics.

At dinner, the nature and properties of everything they eat are explained and discussed, bread, wine, salt, meat, fruit, etc. The sources of this knowledge are Pliny, Dioscorides, and others. After eating, teacher and pupil clean their teeth with care, wash their hands and their eyes, and sit down to a game of dice or arithmetic. Then they sing 'à plaisir de gorge'. Gymnaste takes over from Ponocrates for the various physical exercises of the afternoon, after which they go to the mountains for some well-needed fresh air, and shout like the devil to exercise throat and lungs. Further massage and a change of clothes follow after a leisurely walk back home, stopping occasionally to examine a tree or pick up a flower. The evening meal is much larger than the midday repast:

> son disner estoit sobre et frugal, car tant seulement mangeoit pour refrener les haboys de l'estomach; mais le soupper estoit copieux et large, car tant en prenoit que luy estoit besoing à soy entretenir et nourrir, ce qui est la vraye diète prescripte par l'art de bonne et seure médicine, quoy qu'un tas de badaulx médicins, herseléz en l'officine des sophistes, conseillent le contraire. Durant icelluy repas estoit continuée la leçon du disner tant que bon sembloit; le reste estoit consommé en bons propous, tous lettréz et utiles. (Ibid.)

> his dinner was sober and frugal, for he only ate enough to stay the gnawings of his stomach; but his supper was copious and large, for then he took all that he needed to stay and nourish himself. This is the proper regimen prescribed by the art of good, sound medicine, although a rabble of foolish physicians, worn out by the wranglings of the sophists, advise the contrary. During this meal, the dinner-time lesson was continued for as long as seemed right, the rest of the time being spent in good, learned and profitable conversation.

They then sing, or play musical instruments for the remainder of the evening, 'faisans grand chère' and amusing themselves until bedtime.

ON EDUCATION

> quelquefoys alloient visiter les compaignies des gens lettréz, ou de gens que eussent veu pays estranges.
>
> (Ibid.)
>
> sometimes they went to seek the society of scholars or of men who had visited foreign lands.

The routine is not as rigid and inflexible as it might seem. On rainy days, for example, they take advantage of their enforced period indoors to study art and architecture, to truss hay and cut wood. They might sometimes venture to a goldsmith's or an apothecary, to learn their art at first-hand. On days such as these, their evening meal should be lighter than usual,

> affin que l'intempérie humide de l'air, communicqué au corps par nécessaire confinité, feust par ce moyen corrigée.
>
> (*Gargantua*, XXIV)
>
> as a method of correcting the humid inclemency of the air, communicated to the body by necessary proximity.

Then, if the weather is exceedingly good, they will take a day off for a long excursion.

The accent throughout is on liberty, absence of restriction, and enjoyment. Gargantua's education is made a pleasure to be welcomed, not a burden to be endured. As Rabelais says,

> mieulx resembloit un passetemps de roy que l'estude d'un escholier.
>
> (Ibid.)
>
> it was more like a king's recreation than a student's plan of study

However much of an improvement this may be over the Sorbonne methods, there are some shortcomings which we should noways seek to remove.

(a) the role of memory is still disproportionate. Ponocrates requires his pupil to learn by heart much of the day's lesson.

(b) the programme is too vast, too ambitious. Psychologically, the attempt to absorb so much learning might be damaging to a child, even if it were possible to achieve. The fact that Gargantua is a giant, with presumably a larger brain than the rest of us, is not relevant in these chapters, where Rabelais himself forgets the size of his hero. He clearly regards his Humanist syllabus as feasible.

(c) there is a notable absence of independent work. Even for his revision, the pupil is guided by the ever-present tutor. At no point is Gargantua left alone to ruminate, make personal choices, indulge a whim for solitary study.

In spite of all this, Rabelais's ideas on education (which he did not invent, but which reflect current Humanist thought on the subject, and are the best exposé that exists), represent an enormous advance on the stagnant methods still employed when he was himself a child.

5
Les Petits Moynetons

Rabelais's work contains a powerful criticism of monastic life. He satirizes with vigour the absurdity of the monastic institution, dismisses with scorn the stupidity of the monks, whom he calls 'les petits moynetons' (little monklings). He denounces the monks for their debauchery, drunkenness, lethargy, greed. In this he echoes the fierce attacks upon the monasteries which had been common even in the Middle Ages. But more particularly he is concerned with their culpable ignorance, their uselessness, their worship of the countless saints whose protection they invoke, and the harm which ensues from the power they wield.

A. Their Ignorance

In Chapter XL of *Gargantua*, 'Why monks are shunned by the world', Rabelais compares monks to monkeys, reproaching them for their mechanical, mindless, nauseating jargon, which even they do not understand:

> Ilz marmonnent grand renfort de légendes et pseaulmes nullement par eulx entenduz; ilz content force patenostres, entrelardéz de longs *Ave Mariaz*, sans y penser ny entendre, et ce que je appelle mocque-dieu, non oraison.
>
> (*Gargantua*, XL)

They mumble through ever so many miracle stories and psalms which they don't in the least understand. They count over a number of Paternosters interlarded with long Ave-Marias, without understanding them or giving them so much as a thought; and that I call not prayer, but mockery of God.

In a very vivid phrase, Lucien Febvre has characterized the kind of monk that Rabelais wishes to satirize as a 'diseur nasillard de messes et de prières, égreneur mécanique de patenôtres.[1]'

What is even more reproachful is that the monks are complacent in their ignorance; they have no wish to understand at all:

> En nostre abbaye nous ne estudions jamais, de peur des auripeaux. Nostre feu abbé disoit que c'est chose monstrueuse veoir un moyne sçavant.
> (*Gargantua*, XXXIX)

> In our abbey we never study, for fear of the mumps. Our late abbot used to say that it's a monstrous thing to see a learned monk.

Wallowing in wilful stupidity, the monks use as their prop and defence a rigid formalism which they neither comprehend nor seek to improve. It matters not, in their eyes, that the populace cannot follow their nonsensical babblings either. Rabelais calls them, with manifest annoyance, 'des prescheurs décretalistes'.
(*Gargantua*, XLII)

B. Their Uselessness

It is important to Rabelais the Humanist that men should work for the enlightenment and well-being of mankind in general. Hence his disgust with the congenital laziness of the monks he describes, and with their complete lack of any social purpose:

> un moyne (j'entends de ces ocieux moynes) ne laboure comme le paisant, ne guarde le pays comme l'homme de

[1] *Le Problème de l'Incroyance au XVIe siède*, p. 236.

guerre, ne guerist les malades comme le médecin, ne
presche ny endoctrine le monde comme le bon docteur
évangélicque et pédagoge, ne porte les commoditéz et
choses nécessaires à la républicque comme le marchant.
Ce est la cause pourquoy de tous sont huéz et abhorrys.

(*Gargantua*, XL)

A monk – I mean one of these lazy monks – doesn't till the fields
like a peasant, nor guard the country like a soldier, nor cure the
sick like a physician, nor preach and instruct the world like a good
gospeller and preceptor, nor carry commodities and things that the
public need like a merchant. That is the reason why everyone hoots
at them and abhors them.

C. The Saints

The monasteries helped to multiply the number of saints who
were invoked at the slightest excuse for protection or deliver-
ance, to the extent that the saints were worshipped with more
zeal than God Himself. This can sometimes be very funny, as
when the monks of Seuilly, frightened by the enemy, seem to get
their saints hopelessly confused:

Les pauvres diables de moynes ne sçavaient auquel de
leurs saints se vouer.   (*Gargantua*, XXVII)

The poor devils of monks did not know which of their saints to
turn to.

But the matter ceases to be joke, and becomes an iniquitous
anachronism when the saints are credited with devilish as well
as divine power. Saint Sebastian, for example, is exhorted to
deliver the people from the plague which he has inflicted upon
them:

– O (dist Grandgousier) pauvres gens, estimez vous que la
peste vienne de sainct Sebastian?
– Ouy vrayement (respondit Lasdaller), noz prescheurs
nous l'afferment.

– Ouy? (dist Grandgousier) lez faulz prophètes vous annoncent ilz telz abuz? Blasphèment ilz en ceste façon les justes et sainctz de Dieu qu'ilz les font semblables aux diables, qui ne font que mal entre les humains. . . .
. . . La peste ne tue que le corps, mais telz imposteurs empoisonnent les âmes.   (*Gargantua*, XLV)

Oh, said Grandgousier, you poor creatures. Do you imagine that the plague comes from Saint Sebastian?
– Yes, of course, replied Wearybones, our preachers assure us that it does.
– Indeed? said Grandgousier. Do the false prophets tell you such lies, then? Do they blaspheme God's holy saints in this fashion, making them seem like devils who do men nothing but harm? . . . Pestilence kills only the body, but these impostors poison the soul.

This passage forms part of the chapter on the pilgrims who are journeying towards the shrine of Saint Sebastian. The popularity of pilgrimages was a side-effect of the cult of saints which Rabelais likewise considers socially useless. Grandgousier advises the pilgrims to go back home and look after their families, to work, to educate their children, not to waste their time traipsing across the country on a fool's errand:

ne soyez faciles à ces otieux et inutilles voyages.   (Ibid.)

don't be so ready to undertake these idle, useless journeys in future.

D. Their Harmful Influence

Were the monks really confined to their monasteries and allowed to pursue their idiocies in seclusion, their cretinous ideas would matter little. But unfortunately their pernicious influence is spread far afield, and thereby incurs the wrath, and not just the mockery, of Rabelais. He detests the arrogance with which they claim to be more holy than the common people, merely by virtue of their command of formalistic jargon, and abhors the inference that honest worship must necessarily be expressed in incomprehensible gibberish. In fact, these 'ocieux moynes' reduce God to their own level. They are:

> un tas de papelards et faulx prophètes, qui ont par constitutions humaines et inventions dépravées envenimé tout le monde.
> (*Pantagruel*, XXIX)

> that rabble of popelings and false prophets who have by human imaginations and depraved inventions poisoned the whole world.

They should not meddle in matters outside their proper sphere of influence, such as to make pronouncements on marriage, which should be solely the concern of parents:

> la tyrannicque praesumption d'iceulx redoubtéz taulpetiers, qui ne se contiennent dedans les treillis de leurs mystérieux temples et se entremettent des négoces contraire par diamètre entier à leurs estatz.
> (*Tiers Livre*, XLVIII)

> the tyrannical presumption of these dreaded molecatchers, who do not confine themselves within the bars of their mysterious temples but meddle with matters utterly foreign to their condition.

Owing to their privileged position, the monastic fraternity offers an example to the rest of the people. It is Rabelais's business to point out that the example is a bad one. By their attachment to the outer trappings of religious tradition, by their hypocrisy in preaching abstinence yet indulging in gluttony and debauchery, by their spurious and harmful advice, they are an insult to God and to honest Christians alike.[1]

---

[1] A. J. Krailsheimer has reminded us that Rabelais inherits this critical attitude towards monks who abuse their position, from his Franciscan training at Fontenay. The Franciscans had 'an almost obsessive preoccupation with spiritual wickedness in high places'.

6
On Religion

Rabelais's religious views are stated, by implication, in his educational programme, and in his satire on the monasteries. We have seen that Ponocrates' pupil is required to read the Gospels, *understand* them, and absorb their spirit of charity. We have also seen that Rabelais has little time for the outward manifestations of piety, the solemn and ridiculous mechanical rites which accompany religious orthodoxy. It would be safe to assume, on this evidence alone, that Rabelais prefers an inward, spiritual, private religion, based on feelings, not ceremony. Fortunately, Rabelais gives us much more than this. There is no series of chapters devoted to a discussion of religious matters (as there is for educational views), no coherent system formally presented. But there are hundreds of paragraphs, scattered throughout the books, which, in their transparent clarity, make Rabelais's religious ideas indisputable. And yet they have been disputed.

Were we to rely solely on the evidence of Rabelais's writing, the question of his religious position would be easy to resolve. But the matter is complicated by the fact that Rabelaisian scholars of the greatest authority have debated the colour and nature of Rabelais's Christianity for the better part of a hundred years, and the possibilities which they raise have to be considered.

There are those who say that Rabelais's stories conceal a mockery of God which is at the least blasphemous, and at the most rationalistic. Abel Lefranc goes so far as to see in Rabelais a militant atheist. Lefranc presents the student with the cruellest

ON RELIGION

dilemma; as the greatest Rabelaisian scholar of all time, who devoted at least fifty years of his life to the study of Rabelais, and unearthed most of the important discoveries which we now take for granted, Lefranc earns our deepest gratitude and respect. Then we are confused when we find that one of his conclusions purports to show Rabelais a dangerous and audacious free-thinker, a conclusion which comes as an almighty shock if we have just read Rabelais himself.

There are those who see Rabelais as a Reformer, in the manner of Calvin. The difficulty here is that, before about 1550, it was impossible to tell who was Réformé and who was not, so confusing and intermingled were opinions on the matter, sometimes in opposition to each other, sometimes in close agreement. Certainly before the publication of Calvin's *Institution Chrétienne* in 1536, the Reform was so embryonic and fragmented that it could hardly be said to exist as a 'movement'. Rabelais wrote his *Pantagruel* and *Gargantua* in 1532 and 1534, before the Réformés had a peg on which to hang their ideas, but while these ideas were in wide circulation. There is some evidence in Rabelais's text that he shared them.

Other critics place Rabelais in the category of Pré-Réformé, among those thinkers who wanted to see the Church put its own house in order, peacefully and without interference from outside. Still others refuse to see in Rabelais any hint of the slightest unorthodoxy, finding his blasphemies and his virulent attacks against the Church to be simple jokes, which were so common among the clergy as to be completely without revolutionary significance. Prominent among these is Lucien Febvre, who has devoted a whole book[1] to the refutation of Lefranc's thesis.

Before we examine these various aspects of Rabelais's faith, we must first dispose of two red herrings:

1. It was not possible *not* to be Christian in 1532. One was Christian as one was dark or fair, Lyonnais or Parisian: it was a

[1] *Le Problème de l'Incroyance au XVIe Siècle.*

bald statement of fact, useless to contradict. You were born a Christian, you married as a Christian, you died as a Christian, without choice and as a matter of course. Even if you were to deny God on your deathbed, you would be buried a Christian. So, although we can now discuss whether Rabelais was atheist, Reformist, or Evangelist, the categories are of our making; they did not present themselves as mutually exclusive in his time – they were all Christian. (Even the word 'atheist' was a Christian insult, which carried a meaning rather different from the one it would carry today. One was 'athée' within the framework of Christianity, not outside it.)

2. The scientific and geographical discoveries of the Renaissance did not produce the immediate philosophical revolution which we, in retrospect, tend to think they ought to have produced. With the hindsight of an historical eye, we now see the events of the Renaissance telescoped into a composite mass, with a beginning and an end. Living in the France of 1532, Rabelais was in the middle of it; the full impact of the philosophical repercussions which were to derive from the Renaissance had yet to be felt. At that time, the discovery of the New World was greeted with interest, but no more, and the Copernican theory that the earth revolved around the sun was curious and fascinating, but was slow to upset religious beliefs. Philosophical views and metaphysical beliefs, which now appear incompatible, could then exist side by side.

A. Blasphemy

1. Sitio

In the Chapter on *Les Propos des Bien Yvres* (*Gargantua*, V), one of the drunkards says:

> J'ai la parolle de Dieu en bouche: *Sitio*.

> I have the Gospel word on my tongue: *Sitio*, I thirst.

Sitio was the last word spoken by Christ on the cross. By placing this same revered word in the mouth of an inebriated fool, Rabelais lays himself open to the charge of blasphemy. Perhaps. But it was a blasphemy which shocked no one. To make fun of this word was, according to Lucien Febvre, the oldest joke of all, a cliché among the clergy. Furthermore, Rabelais did not insert this word into his text until 1542. It is absent from the first edition of 1534, and only appears in the second edition, from which Rabelais wished to expurgate some of his more offensive satires. He could hardly, then, have considered this a particular dangerous blasphemy.

2. Gargantua's strange birth

Gargantua does not come into the world in the customary fashion, but exits from his mother's body through her left ear. Anticipating the reader's disbelief, Rabelais interrupts his narrative to say:

> Je me doubte que ne croyez asseurément ceste estrange nativité. Si ne le croyez, je ne m'en soucie, mais un homme de bien, un homme de bon sens, croit tousjours ce qu'on luy dict et qu'il trouve par escript.
>
> (*Gargantua*, VI)

> I doubt whether you will truly believe in this strange nativity. I don't care if you don't. But an honest man, a man of good sense, always believes what he is told and what he finds written down.

In the 1534 edition, the passage was slightly more provocative, with the additional sentence, 'Les Sorbonnistes disent que foy est argument des choses de nulle apparence.'

This has been said to be a blasphemous reference to the Virgin Birth of Jesus Christ; if you can believe that, implies Rabelais, then you should believe the no more ridiculous birth of Gargantua. The parallel is misleading; Rabelais does not claim that Gargantua's birth is miraculous, nor does he suggest for a moment that Christ was born through Mary's ear. To be truly blasphemous, the analogy would need to be closer than it is. Rabelais is not mocking the text of the Bible, but those 'Sorbonnistes' who exploit that text to their advantage, and allow no academic research into the sacred book.

3. *Mammallement scandaleuse*

To nourish her giant son, Gargamelle had to draw from her breasts 'fourteen hundred and two pipes and nine pails of milk at a time', according to certain Scotist doctors. With mock seriousness, Rabelais says that he thinks this highly unlikely and concludes that the suggestion is:

> mammallement scandaleuse, des pitoyables aureilles offensives, et sentent de loing hérésie.
>
> (*Gargantua*, VII)
>
> mammalianly scandalous, offensive to pious ears, and distantly redolent of heresy.

These words are a parody of the official formula of condemnation used so frequently by the Sorbonne. As such, they amount only to a gentle but sarcastic mockery of theologians.

4. *Pantagruel's Pedigree*

Chapter One of *Pantagruel* consists of a long and amusing list of the giant's ancestors, written in the style of Biblical genealogy:

> Et le premier fut Chalbroth,
> Qui engendra Sarabroth,
> Qui engendra Faribroth,

and so on for three or four pages. The parody is so apparent, that it would be useless to deny it. But, here again, there was nothing new, unusual or shocking in having fun at the expense of Genesis or St Matthew. The friars amused themselves regularly in this way without ever being suspected of blasphemy; and Rabelais was not the first to use the joke in print.

There are other instances of Rabelais the mocker of Biblical style. In enumerating the victims of a disaster, he frequently concludes the list with the words 'sans les femmes et petits enfants', an obvious parody of a much-used Biblical formula.

5. The 'Resurrection' of Epistémon

After the battle led by Pantagruel against Loup-Garou, Epistémon, whose head has been cut off by a stone, lies bleeding and apparently dead. The company bemoan his loss, but Panurge says that the body is still warm and can be saved. Whereupon Panurge knits the tissues and veins together, and Epistémon is soon restored to full vigour.

Abel Lefranc considers this passage to be blasphemous: 'Notre conviction absolue est qu'on se trouve ici en présence d'une parodie des deux miracles les plus considérables du Nouveau Testament, à savoir: la résurrection de la fille de Jaïre et celle de Lazare.'

The parallels between this harmless little anecdote, which offers Rabelais yet another opportunity of displaying his medical knowledge, and the miracle of Lazarus's resurrection, are thin indeed. Had Rabelais intended a blasphemy here, he would surely have made it more obvious, as was his wont. In this instance, Abel Lefranc has been carried away by his own erudition. It is more likely that Rabelais merely wished to mock the fraudulent miracles which were a daily occurence in the Middle Ages.

B. Atheist

We have already had cause to refer to the charges of impiety which beset Rabelais most of his life, and to his cry of anger against them in the dedicatory preface to the *Quart Livre* (cf.

Chapter One). When Abel Lefranc published the Champion edition of *Pantagruel* in the early years of this century, he went much further than any of the sixteenth-century slanderers had done. He discerned in Rabelais's writings a 'secret' thought of 'une audace à peine concevable', lurking beneath the apparently light-hearted tone of the narrative. The gay pleasantries concealed a strange purpose which nobody (before Lefranc) had dared to imagine possible. Nobody had thought to question whether Rabelais had ceased to be a Christian. Lefranc poses the question, and offers the startling answer that 'l'auteur de ce livre a adhéré, au début de sa carrière littéraire, à la foi rationaliste, à ce que les modernes appellent la pensée indépendante'. Lefranc makes of Rabelais a propagandist, the leader of a covert band of free-thinkers, 'S'il a composé *Pantagruel*, c'est qu'il prétendait atteindre, par cette oeuvre, tous ceux qui à travers le monde rêvaient d'une émancipation religieuse totale.'[1]

Febvre's view could not be more opposed. He finds no evidence of the audacity which Lefranc proclaims: 'on hésite à trouver Rabelais audacieux. On est assez près de le juger timide'. Febvre maintains that Lefranc's mistake derives from a fundamental misunderstanding of the sixteenth century: 'J'ai un peu peur, faut-il le dire, qu'Abel Lefranc ne se soit laissé égarer par une notion trop sommaire de ce qu'était un chrétien . . . et un Français des années 1530.'[2]

How has the dispute arisen? What is the evidence which might support a theory of Rabelaisian atheism? There are, first of all, the various blasphemies, some of which are referred to above, and which are finally quite innocent. Then there is the fact that many were the contemporaries who accused Rabelais of atheism. Lefranc quotes half a dozen of them. Febvre points out that some do not refer to Rabelais at all, and that anyway, the word 'athée' had no strict meaning, but was hurled indiscriminately as a pejorative epithet in much the same way as

[1] *Rabelais,* pp. 179, 180, 190, 191, 193, 196, 203.
[2] *Le Problème de L'Incroyance* . . ., pp. 154, 156.

ON RELIGION

'communist' is sometimes used today. 'Il n'avait pas un sens strictement défini. Il s'employait dans le sens qu'on voulait bien lui donner.' In fact, 'athée' was little more than a swear-word.

A swear-word used by all and sundry, moreover! Dolet was accused of atheism (with far more reason than Rabelais), and in turn accused Erasmus of atheism. Rabelais himself, in the very year in which *Pantagruel* first appeared, accused Scaliger of atheism. The text is a letter addressed to Bernard de Salignac and dated 30 November 1532:

> c'est un calomniateur qui, à vrai dire, n'est pas ignorant en médecine, mais quant au reste aussi parfaitement athée que personne le fut jamais.[1]

As Febvre says, 'ces athées paraissent assez enclins à se scandaliser de l'athéisme d'autrui'. The truth of the matter is that none of these writers was as objective or precise in his choice of words as we would be today.[2] The twentieth-century concept of atheism does not belong to the sixteenth century in France.

Another insult frequently used among authors was 'Lucianiste'. Lefranc makes much of this epithet which compares Rabelais to the great Greek satirist, and he quotes from Calvin ('des chiens enragéz qui desgorgent leurs ordures à l'encontre de la majesté de Dieu, et ont voulu pervertir toute religion'), Robert Estienne, and Henri Estienne. Again, Febvre points out that the word was a generic term, applied to any writer whose wit rose above the mediocre. It had been said of Erasmus, and of Bonaventure des Périers: 'C'est un nom de famille. Ce n'est pas un nom d'individu.'[3]

The argument is far more detailed than we have been able to show in this quick summary. Lefranc observes that there is no chapel mentioned in the account of the Abbaye de Thélème.

---

[1] In the Pléiade edition, p. 966.
[2] *Le Problème de l'Incroyance*. . . ., pp. 127, 128, 129, 130, 142.
[3] *Rabelais*, pp. 198–200. *Le Problème de l'Incroyance*, p. 65.

Febvre replies that there is no kitchen either. So what? Et ainsi de suite.

To conclude, there is evidence exterior to the texts which should be taken into account. In the first place, Rabelais had been a friar, and was now a secular priest. It is quite possible, even probable, that he preached. This would have been gratuitous hypocrisy for a down-to-earth atheist. Secondly, Rabelais was protected throughout his literary career by a total of three cardinals. They presumably knew what they were doing, and unless they were hypocrites too, would not have protected an atheist whose 'secret' thoughts appear to have been broadcast widely by his enemies.

The kernel of the problem is to learn how to read Rabelais as a sixteenth-century writer, to see him as his contemporaries saw him, and then everything falls into place. Despite his immense authority, Abel Lefranc, in the opinion of his critics, has been guilty of a distorted perspective. As Etienne Gilson rather unkindly put it: 'Il faut se mettre en état de comprendre les textes avant de les commenter.' In a sixteenth-century context, the supposedly atheistic passages in Rabelais's work amount to little more than the amusing, sometimes barbed pleasantries of a Humanist who saw much that was wrong with the Church, who detested ritual and pretension, who lamented the example set by the monasteries, who enjoyed hackneyed jokes at the expense of the Bible, but who nevertheless believed himself to be, and who was, a Christian.

C. Immortality

The first four paragraphs of Gargantua's letter to Pantagruel (*Pantagruel*, VIII), express the father's desire to live on in his son after his own death. Death is the punishment we have inherited for the sin of Adam and Eve, says Gargantua, but our departing from this world is made less painful by our ability to leave behind physical characteristics and personality traits which survive in our children and in generations to follow. Knowing the weaknesses and vanities of human nature, God has bestowed upon us this gift of genetic inheritance as a kind of palliative; it is a way to achieve a semblance of immortality in this world:

> (l'humaine nature) peut en estat mortel acquérir espèce de immortalité et, en décours de vie transitoire, perpétuer son nom et sa semence ... par ce moyen de propogation séminale demeure ès enfans ce que estoit déperdu ès parents.
>
> we can, in this mortal state, acquire a kind of immortality and, in the course of this transitory life, perpetuate our name and seed ... by this method of seminal propagation, there remains in the children what has perished in the parents.

The process will continue until the Day of Judgement, when death will cease, and procreation of the species will no longer be necessary.

Gargantua is happy to think that his son will perpetuate his name on this earth:

> je rends grâces à Dieu, mon conservateur, de ce qu'il m'a donné povoir veoir mon antiquité chanue refleurir en ta jeunesse; car, quand par le plaisir de luy, qui tout régist et modère, mon âme laissera ceste habitation humaine, je ne me réputeray totallement mourir, ains passer d'un lieu en aultre, attendu que en toy et par toy je demeure en mon image visible en ce monde, vivant, voyant, et conversant entre gens de honneur et mes amys comme je souloys.
>
> I offer thanks to God, my Preserver, for permitting me to see my grey-haired age blossom afresh in your youth. When, at the will of Him who rules and governs all things, my soul shall leave this mortal habitation, I shall not now account myself to be absolutely dying, but to be passing from one place to another, since in you, and by you, I shall remain in visible form here in this world, visiting and conversing with men of honour and my friends as I used to do.

Abel Lefranc has analysed this passage in some detail, and has concluded that it is the work of one who denies the Christian doctrine of the Immortality of the Soul. Nowhere, says Lefranc, is the immortality of the soul in an afterlife so much as mentioned, and the use of the words 'totallement mourir', suggesting that death is the end of something, rather than the beginning, reflect a dangerous impiety.

There are several objections to this view:

1. Words very similar to 'totallement mourir' were used by other authors who could not by any stretch of the imagination be suspected of impiety. Febvre quotes a passage from Bossuet, for example, which echoes the sentiments of Gargantua.

2. Gargantua does not mention the immortality of the soul because that is not his subject, in this letter. He is talking about something which is utterly different, the pride and satisfaction which a father may derive from his son's success. The letter goes on to say that *because* you, Pantagruel, will be my earthly representative after my death, I want you to take every advantage to study, to gain wisdom and maturity.

3. There are other passages where Rabelais does discuss the immortality of the soul, and which should be read alongside Gargantua's letter. For example:

> En ceste façon nostre âme, lors que le corps dort, . . . s'esbat et reveoit sa patrie qui est le ciel.
>
> (*Tiers Livre*, XIII)

In this way, once your body is sleeping . . . the soul enjoys itself and revisits its own country, which is the heavens.

Or again:

> Je croy, dist Pantagruel, que toutes âmes intellectives sont exemptes des ciseaulx de Atropos. Toutes sont immortelles: Anges, Daemons et Humaines.
>
> (*Quart Livre*, XXVII)

ON RELIGION

> I believe that all intellectual souls are exempt from the scissors of Atropos, said Pantagruel. They are all immortal, whether angelic, demonic, or human.

The student should also read the *Almanach pour l'an 1535*,[1] in which Rabelais states that man's insatiable desire to learn and to know more are a conclusive indication of the immortality of the soul. For our desires in this direction can only be satisfied, and will be satisfied, when we have left this life and joined Christ in the other.

D. Reformist?

While Rabelais was writing his first two books, the Reform in France was still incipient; few people desired, and none foresaw, the rupture with the Church of Rome. Fervent religious feeling impelled many Humanists to exhort the Church to reform itself. Rabelais shared this feeling, and gave expression to it in his work.

In the first place, he has much to say about the temporal power of the Pope. The chapters of the *Quart Livre* which deal with the Papimanes are a powerful satire on the superstitious idolatry which surrounds the Pope, and on the *Décrétales*, articles of Papal law which enforce the secular power of Rome. In Chapter LIII the immense wealth of the Vatican is attacked, together with the corrupt political methods of accumulating it.

Rabelais returns to the attack in the *Cinquième Livre*. (Although the authorship of this last book is contested, it is quite possible that Rabelais wrote the first chapters, originally published under the title *L'Isle Sonante*). The Ringing Island clangs with the persistant noise of hundreds of bells. It is inhabited by birds who differ from men only in their plumage, 'lequel aucuns avoient tout blanc, autres tout noir, autres tout gris, autres mi-parti de blanc et noir, autres tout rouge, autres

[1] In the Pléiade edition, p. 907.

parti de blanc et bleu'. They are variously called Clergaulx, Monesgaux, Prestregaulx, Abbégaulx, and so on, with an obvious reference to clerical hierarchy, and at their head is one Papegault. Rabelais goes on to satirize the magistrates, whom he calls 'les Chats-fourrés'.

Satire of this kind was typical of Reformist attacks on the Church. It would be wrong to suppose, however, that Rabelais can thereby be categorized as a Reformist. His attacks against Calvin and his followers show an equal disdain:

> les Démoniacles Calvins, imposteurs de Genève.
> (*Quart Livre*, XXXII)

Rabelais may perhaps have felt in sympathy with the Calvinists at the beginning of his literary career, but such sympathy had certainly evaporated before the publication of the *Quart Livre*. After all, there was much in Calvinist doctrine which was profoundly repugnant to Rabelais.

While orthodox catholicism maintained that salvation was a reward which God bestowed upon good Christians, that one could therefore earn one's place in Paradise by the performance of good deeds, and that earthly goods were consequently of no value, Calvinist doctrine insisted, on the contrary, that good deeds could not guarantee salvation. One could only be saved by the grace of God, which was given indiscriminately and gratuitously, without reference to just deserts or meritorious actions. You cannot *earn* salvation, said the Calvinists, but you may receive it as a free gift if you are lucky. Meanwhile, God will show some indication in advance of who are his favoured people, by allowing them to become rich and successful in this world.

Such a doctrine was rigidly deterministic and profoundly hopeless. Austere pessimism of this sort did not appeal to Rabelais. Moreover, it encouraged self-indulgence (Rabelais characterized the Calvinists as fat and self-satisfied). Worse still, there is no place for morals in a system which dictates that divine grace pays no attention to the actions of men. Rabelais, as we shall see later, attaches much importance to morals and ethical conduct. He refuses the notion of an Original Sin which perverts human nature irrevocably. Austerity was not to his liking. Indeed, if one must compare him with anyone, Rabelais is closer to Erasmus than to Calvin, and in many respects echoes Erasmian thought.[1] As Paul Stapfer has written: 'Il est partisan de la Réforme dans la mesure où celle-ci est l'allié des belles Lettres et l'émancipatrice de la pensée, mais il n'a garde de suivre Calvin dans sa négation désespérante du libre-arbitre et sa sombre doctrine de la prédestination.'

E. Rabelais's Faith

Rabelais is no theoretician, no theologian. Not once does he set forth a coherent system of religious ideas. Yet the expression of confident religious faith is the single most recurrent theme in his whole work. It is impossible not to be moved by the lyricism and elegance with which he expresses a simple, strong, tenacious faith in a God who is omnipotent, omniscient, benign, the personification of Goodness.

1. Omnipotence

The God of Rabelais is the Creator of Heaven and Earth, the beginning and end of all being:

> Dieu le créateur, lequel par sa divine parolle tout régist et modère, par laquelle sont toutes choses en leur nature et propriété et condition, et sans la maintenance et gouvernement duquel toutes choses seroient en un moment réduictes à néant, comme de néant elles ont esté par luy produictes en leur estre. *(Pantagruéline Prognostication)*

---

[1] cf. Febvre, *Le Problème de l'Incroyance. . . .*, pp. 300–2.

> God the Creator, who rules and governs everything by His divine word, which maintains the nature, property and condition of all things, and without whose control all things would be in an instant reduced to nothingness, as they were from nothingness created by Him. (*My translation*.)

He created the stars, the moon, all the empirical world which surrounds us, everything which we see, feel, and are. He 'tout a créé et dispensé selon son sacré arbitre.' (*Almanach pour 1535*)

> Tout, tout ce que sommes, tout ce que vivons, tout ce que avons, tout ce que espérons est luy, en luy, de luy, par luy.
> (*Quart Livre,* XXVIII)

> He is our All, all that we are, all that we live by, all that we have, all that we hope for is from him, in him, of him, and by him. [The reference is to Pan, but a Christian interpretation is clearly intended.]

Thus, God has infinite power. There is hardly a chapter in which Rabelais does not celebrate, at some point, divine omnipotence. His will is impenetrable and limitless. His being immutable and eternal.

He is also omniscient. He sees and understands everything, nothing can be hidden from His view. When Gallet is sent as emissary by Grandgousier to remonstrate with the aggressor Picrochole, he exclaims:

> Où est foy? Où est loy? Où est raison? Où est humanité? Où est craincte de Dieu? Cuyde tu ces oultraiges estre recellez as esperitz éternelz et au Dieu souverain qui est juste rétributeur de noz entreprinses? Si le cuyde, tu te trompe car toutes choses viendront à son jugement.
> (*Gargantua,* XXXI)

> Where is faith? Where is law? Where is reason? Where is humanity? Where is the fear of God? Do you think that these wrongs are concealed from the eternal spirits and from Almighty God, who is the just rewarder of all our undertakings? If you think so, you are deceived, for all things will come before His judgement.

ON RELIGION

As law-giver and judge, God is to be respected and obeyed; His precepts must be followed:

> aymant et craignant Dieu, aymant complaire à Dieu par foy et observation de ses saincts commandemens, craignant l'offenser et perdre sa grâce par défault de foy et transgression de sa divine loy.
> (*Tiers Livre*, XXX)

> who loves to please God by faith and the observance of His holy commandments, who fears to offend Him and lose His favour through faithlessness and the transgression of His divine law.

2. Grace and Free Will

We are powerless to do God's will without the benefit of His divine grace, which guides and protects us. Hippothadée tells Panurge in the *Tiers Livre* that we are worthless if 'sa saincte grâce n'est sus nous infuse'. Deprived of divine grace, we are left to flounder with our insufficient free will, which leads us only to disaster. Picrochole has been abandoned to his free will:

> Dieu éternel l'a laissé au gouvernail de son franc arbitre et propre sens, qui ne peult estre que meschant sy par grâce divine n'est continuellement guidé.
> (*Gargantua*, XXIX)

> God Almighty has abandoned him to the guidance of his own free will and understanding, which cannot but be evil unless it be continually prompted by divine grace.

Those who think they know better than God, who deny Him and refuse His grace, have strayed from reason into corruption:

> rien n'est ny sainct ny sacré à ceulx qui se sont émancipez de Dieu et Raison pour suivre leurs affections perverses.
> (*Gargantua*, XXXI)

nothing is holy or sacred to those who have emancipated themselves from God and reason to follow their own perverse desires.

Whereas divine grace may be bestowed or withdrawn at God's pleasure, it is not so capricious as the grace described in Calvinist doctrine. For it is given as a reward, and taken away as a punishment. God has abandoned Picrochole to free will as a retribution for his irascibility and aggressiveness. In other words, men must show that they are worthy of God's grace.

3. Benignity and Prayer

God may be powerful, but He is also good. The accent on His goodness is prevalent throughout Rabelais's work. It is to God that the giants address themselves when in physical or moral danger, or when beset by doubt. Prayer therefore plays a pre-eminent role. Grandgousier prays to God when he first learns that Picrochole has invaded his lands:

> mon Dieu, mon Saulveur, ayde moy, inspire moy, conseille moy à ce qu'est de faire! (*Gargantua*, XXVIII)
>
> My God, my Saviour, help me, inspire me, counsel me what I should do.

Later, when Gallet returns from his mission, he finds Grandgousier

> à genoux, teste nue, incliné en un petit coing de son cabinet, priant Dieu qu'il voulsist amollir la cholère de Pichrochole et le mettre au poinct de raison.
>
> (*Gargantua*, XXXII)
>
> on his knees, bareheaded, prostrate in a little corner of his chamber, praying God to moderate Picrochole's anger and to bring him to reason.

Before going into battle with Loup-Garou, Pantagruel implored God to protect him:

ON RELIGION

Seigneur Dieu, qui tousjours as esté mon protecteur et mon Servateur, tu vois la détresse en laquelle je suis maintenant . . .
(*Pantagruel*, XXIX)

O Lord God! Thou has been my protector and my saviour. Thou seest the distress in which I now am.

And we already know that Gargantua's education includes a nightly prayer to God and invocation of His goodness:

Si prioient Dieu le créateur, en l'adorant et ratifiant leur foy envers luy, et le glorifiant de sa bonté immense, et, luy rendant grâce de tout le temps passé, se recommandoient à sa divine clémence pour tout l'advenir.
(*Gargantua*, XXIII)

And so they prayed to God the Creator, worshipping Him, reaffirming their faith in Him, glorifying Him for His immense goodness, rendering thanks to Him for all the past, and recommending themselves to His divine clemency for all the future.

Sincere prayer is always answered. God intervenes in the affairs of men to give aid and assistance, or to forgive transgressions sincerely repented. Rabelais rejects the notion that men are damned from birth by unshakeable sin. His God is infinitely kind, forgiving, protective:

metz tout ton espoir en Dieu et il ne te délaissera poinct . . . toute ma fiance est en Dieu, mon protecteur, lequel jamais ne délaisse ceux qui en luy ont mis leur espoir et pensée.
(*Pantagruel*, XXVII)

Place all your hope in God, and He will not abandon you. . . . All my confidence is in God, my protector, who never abandons those who have placed their hope and reliance in Him.

The greatest good to which men can aspire is to share the afterlife with God and His Son Jesus Christ. Then, earthly passions and petty tribulations will no longer buffet us, as we bathe in His infinite Love:

> Lors cesseront toutes passions, affections et imperfections humaines, car en jouyssance de luy aurons plénitude de tout bien, tout sçavoir et perfection.
>
> (*Almanach pour l'an 1535*)

> Then all passions, desires, and human imperfections will cease, for enjoying Him shall we have fullness of all Good, all Knowledge and perfection. (*My translation.*)

Rabelais's God is above all a *personal* God, to whom his heroes turn in time of need, who listens and advises, protects and comforts, punishes or forgives. He is far removed from the austere God of Calvin.

4. *The Gospels*

> Le bon Dieu nous a faict ce bien qu'il nous les a révéléz, annoncéz, déclairéz et apertement descriptz par les sacres bibles.
>
> (*Tiers, Livre*, XXX)

> The good God has done us the favour of revealing, announcing, declaring, and openly stating His pleasure to us in the Holy Scriptures.

This quotation is taken from the passage in which Hippothadée advises Panurge on the choice of a wife. According to Abel Lefranc, Hippothadée is based on Lefèvre d'Étaples, the great Humanist whom Rabelais admired, and who taught that in the Scriptures was found the only true expression of Christian doctrine. As a Humanist, Rabelais shares this view. His work is scattered with references to the 'saint Évangile' and to 'le bon apôtre Saint Paul'. It is Saint Paul that he quotes when he writes:

ON RELIGION

> Tous vrays christians, de tous estatz, en tous lieux, en tous temps, prient Dieu, et l'Esperit prie et intercelle pour iceulx, et Dieu les prent en grâce.　　　(*Gargantua*, XL)
>
> All true Christians, of all degrees, in all places, and at all times, pray to God, and the Holy Spirit prays and intercedes for them, and God receives them into His grace.

(This is one of the very few references, incidentally, to the third element of the Trinity.) By returning to the Holy Scriptures, to the Gospels, the wrong-headed interpretations imposed by the Church can be swept aside, and God's word revealed in its purity:

> je feray prescher ton sainct Évangile purement, simplement et entièrement, si que les abus d'un tas de papelars et faulx prophètes, qui ont par constitutions humaines et inventions dépravées envenimé tout le monde, seront d'entour moy exterminéz.　　　(*Pantagruel*, XXIX)
>
> I will cause thy Holy Gospel to be preached purely, simply, and in its entirety, so that the abuses of that rabble of popelings and false prophets who have by human imaginations and depraved inventions poisoned the whole world shall be exterminated from about me.

The 'constitutions humaines et inventions dépravées' refer to faulty interpretations of the Gospels, to the worship of the Virgin Mary, the pilgrimages, the sale of pardons, and all the other corruptions which Rabelais detested, and which have been discussed earlier.

Grandgousier tells his prisoner Toucquedillon that the invasion he has suffered is contrary to the teaching of the Gospels:

> contraire à la profession de l'Évangile, par lequel nous est commandé guarder, saulver, régir et administrer chascun ses pays et terres, non hostilement envahir les aultres...
> 　　　((*Gargantua*, XLVI)

is contrary to Gospel teaching, by which we are enjoined each to guard, protect, rule and administer his own lands and territories, and not to make hostile attacks on those of others.

and his wife Gargamelle admits that she takes greater pleasure in hearing a piece read to her from the Scriptures, than hearing the tale of Saint Margaret, or 'quelque autre capharderie'. On the very last page of *Gargantua*, the hero laments that those who spread the word of the Gospel are still persecuted:

> Ce n'est de maintenant que les gens réduitz à la créance évangélicque sont persécutez.
>
> (*Gargantua*, LVIII)

This is not the first time that men called to the gospel faith have been persecuted.

The Abbaye de Thélème, Rabelais's imaginary and ideal monastery, carries an inscription above its main door, on which are written words of welcome to the Evangelists:

> Cy entrez, vous, qui le sainct Évangile
> En sens agile annoncez . . .
> Entrez, qu'on fonde icy la foy profonde,
> Puis qu'on confonde, et par voix et par rolle,
> Les ennemys de la saincte parolle.
>
> (*Gargantua*, LIV)

Enter here, you who preach with vigour Christ's Holy Gospel . . . Enter. Here let us found a faith profound, and then let us confound by speech and writing, all that are the foemen of the Holy Writ.

5. *Morality*

Although he is not a theologian, and points of Christian dogma are barely discussed in his work, Rabelais *is* a moralist. He agrees with most Humanists of his period in asserting that religion cannot be separated from morality.

ON RELIGION

> Science sans conscience n'est que ruine de l'âme.
> (*Pantagruel,* VIII)

knowledge without conscience is but the ruin of the soul.

Consequently, many of his chapters are pregnant with ethical maxims of one kind or another, especially in the more serious moments. Gargantua's advice to Pantagruel in the famous letter is a case in point:

> Ne mets ton coeur à vanité, car cette vie est transitoire, mais la parolle de Dieu demeure éternellement.
> (Ibid.)

set not your heart on vanity, for this life is transitory, but the word of God remains eternal.

There are many other examples, as in Gallet's speech to Picrochole, in Grandgousier's speech to the vanquished, and so on.

It is worth pausing to ask why ethical conduct should play such a large part in Rabelais's religion. What is the good of being moral and virtuous if salvation can only be won through the grace of God? Rabelais says that you cannot *earn* salvation by parroting a hundred *Ave Marias* a day, or hiking to some distant shrine, but you can, and should, lay yourself open to receive God's grace by being virtuous, by showing that you are sincere. It is no good waiting for grace to descend upon you; a moral effort is required on your part too. The bestowal of divine grace is the result of a partnership between God and man:

> icelluy (Dieu) fault incessamment implorer, invocquer, prier, requerir, supplier. Mais là ne fault faire but et bourne: de nostre part, convient pareillement nous évertuer, et, comme dict le sainct Envoyé, estre coopérateurs avecques luy.
> (*Quart Livre,* XXIII)

we must unceasingly implore, invoke, pray, beseech and supplicate him. But we must not confine ourselves to that. We must also make efforts on our own account, and, as the Holy Apostle says, be workers together with him.

We find, therefore, that Rabelais's ethics illustrate what can best be described as an *active Evangelism*, the conscious and purposeful performance of good for its own sake. One of the most important maxims in Gargantua's letter is the following:

> Soys serviable à tous tes prochains, et les ayme comme toy mesmes. (*Pantagruel*, VIII)
>
> Be helpful to all your neighbours, and love them as yourself.

Krailsheimer has shown conclusively how Pantagruel's life henceforth is an illustration of this advice put into practice. In the next chapter, Pantagruel meets Panurge, a penniless down-and-out, living only on his wits. Pantagruel's first words to him are:

> Car j'ay affection très grande de vous donner ayde à mon povoir en la calamité où je vous voy; car vous me faictes grand pitié. (*Pantagruel*, IX)
>
> I have a very great desire to give you all the aid in my power in the calamity in which I find you. In fact, I feel great pity for you.

There is no clear reason why Pantagruel, a prince, should befriend Panurge, a beggar, yet they become inseparable companions. Pantagruel wishes to save Panurge from moral penury as he has saved him from material deprivation. Whether his friend is cowardly, cunning, or frightened, Pantagruel never deserts him.

Not only should one love one's friends, but one's enemies also. Each of the books contains the account of a battle, in which an enemy is defeated. Each time, the giants show great magnanimity in their victory, forgive their enemies, assist them to re-establish themselves after defeat. In short, the giants do not take an eye for an eye or a tooth for a tooth; they will not return evil for evil.

Charity is the keynote of the giant's ethical code, a disinterested charity embraced for its own sake, because it is a reflection on earth of divine goodness. Gargantua exhorts his son to abide by a 'foy formée de charité' (*Pantagruel*, VIII), repeating with these words a formula well-known to medieval theology (*fides charitate formata*), and absolutely foreign to Calvinist doctrine. It is in the moral sphere that Rabelais is mostly clearly distinguished from Calvin's Reform.

7

The Naturalism of Rabelais: L'Abbaye de Thélème

A. Human Nature

Rabelais hates all that conspires to stifle the natural flowering of human endeavour – medieval asceticism, lethargy, constraint, ignorance. He exalts all that helps men to realize their potential, to give them free expression of their nature – health, learning, liberty, companionship. For Rabelais, in spite of all the shortcomings which he so keenly observes in men, and which he so joyously satirizes, retains a bright and happy confidence in the fundamental goodness of human nature:

> gens libères, bien néz, bien instruictz, conversans en compaignies honnestes, ont par nature un instinct et aiguillon, qui tousjours les poulse à faictz vertueux et retire du vice, lequel ilz nommoient honneur.
> (*Gargantua*, LVII)

> people who are free, well-born, well-bred, and easy in honest company, have a natural spur and instinct which drives them to virtuous deeds and deflects them from vice; and this they call honour.

He makes the distinction between *Physis* (Nature), from which comes Beauty and Harmony, and *Antiphysie* (Anti-Nature), which gives birth to Discord, Hypocrisy, Immoderation. Abstinence, so important in medieval monasteries, deforms nature and is harmful to health of mind and body alike.

It might seem, on the face of it, that this confidence is incompatible with the religious views examined in the previous chapter. Picrochole, after all, when deprived of divine grace and abandoned to his 'nature', wrought chaos and evil all around him. The contradiction is, however, superficial, and has led to frequent misinterpretation of Rabelaisian naturalism. Human nature, as Rabelais understands it (and here he follows Plato), is synonymous with *Reason*, and reason is the gift of God. Picrochole, deserted by God, is deprived of reason and left to guide his actions only by his passions. Human nature, on the other hand, is desire tempered by virtue, and is godly in its origin; it must not be equated with human passions. The freedom which is necessary to the full expression of human nature is freedom from artificial restrictions invented by man, *not* freedom from God and His laws.

Just as asceticism deforms human nature by its enforced abstinence, so its opposite, greed, deforms nature by its immoderation. Both ascetics and gluttons are self-indulgent; if one may use twentieth-century terms, the former indulge themselves masochistically, the latter orgiastically. Neither obey the 'instinct et aiguillon' provided by reason/human nature. The crime of the *Gastrolâtres*, described in chapter LXI of the *Quart Livre*, is to have loved themselves (by satisfying their gluttony) more than they loved their neighbour. The crime of the ascetics is similar, being satisfied with their own self-deprivation rather than making a moral effort to do good for their fellows.

Rabelais's confidence in human nature is evidence of a glorious *optimism*. One of the fundamental traits of his Humanism is the belief that, though imperfect, man can attain perfection. With the guidance of God and the company of men, says the Divine Bottle (*Cinquième Livre*, XLVII), all knowledge is accessible. And, by implication, contentment. As Rabelais says in his Prologue to the *Tiers Livre*:

> Bon espoir y gist au fond.
>
> good hope lies at the bottom.

If Rabelais can be said to have a 'philosophy', it lies in this supreme confidence in the nature of men to achieve happiness. He himself called it *Pantagruelisme*, a certain attitude towards life which he defines as:

> certaine gayeté d'esprit conficte en mespris des choses fortuites. (Prologue to *Quart Livre*)
>
> a certain lightness of spirit compounded of contempt for the chances of fate.

Pantagruelism is not simply joviality, as it has sometimes been understood, nor a 'gay stoicism', but a philosophic detachment which prevents one being too easily hurt by the accidents of life. It is also a willingness to assume the best of people, to have good will towards men, put the best construction on their motives, be reluctant to think ill of them. Thus, when Grandgousier learns that his lands have been invaded by Picrochole, he immediately assumes that the man is not responsible for his actions, or that there has been some mistake, or that he has been urged and provoked by somebody else. Almost his first words, uttered in bewilderment and shock, are

> Qui le meut? Qui le poinct? Qui le conduict? Qui l'a ainsi conseillé? (*Gargantua*, XXVIII)
>
> Who is inciting him? Who is urging him on? Who is leading him? Who has advised him to do this?

Grandgousier will not believe that Picrochole is capable of evil until it is proven to him. Even then, he will bear him no lasting grudge.

THE NATURALISM OF RABELAIS

The finest incarnation of Pantagruelism is, of course, Pantagruel himself. In a brief character sketch we are told that:

> Pantagruel, adverty de l'affaire, n'en feut en soy aulcunement indigné, fasché ne marry. Je vous ay ja dict et encores rediz que c'estoit le meilleur petit et grand bon hommet qui oncques ceigneit espée. Toutes choses prenoit en bonne partie, tout acte interprétoit à bien. Jamais ne se tourmentoit, jamais ne se scandalizoit. Car tous les biens que le ciel couvre et que la terre contient . . . ne sont dignes d'esmouvoir nos affections et troubler nos sens et espritz.
>
> (*Tiers Livre*, II)

When Pantagruel heard this news he was not in any way indignant, angry, or perturbed. For as I have already told you, and I tell you once more, he was the best little great good fellow that ever wore a sword. He took everything in good part, put favourable interpretation on every act, never tormented himself, and was never scandalized. For all the wealth that the sky covers and earth contains . . . is not worth so much that we should upset our affections [emotions], or trouble our sense and spirits for it.

It is a calm philosophy, in which the virtues of tolerance and understanding flower effortlessly, and the vices of anger, envy, suspicion and impatience are *naturally* withstood. It is the philosophy of Socrates, to whom Rabelais paid homage in his Prologue to *Gargantua* (quoted in Chapter 3), Socrates, whose infinite wisdom endowed him with a 'contempt for all those things men so watch for, pursue, work for, and sail after'. Pantagruelism clearly owes much to the quiet serenity of the Greek philosopher.

B. L'Abbaye de Thélème

Grandgousier establishes the Abbaye de Thélème as a reward for Frère Jean's part in the Picrocholone War. It will be an ideal place, where human nature may flourish in peace, the exact opposite in every detail to the medieval monasteries of reality. It is a kind of anti-monastic monastery:

> requist à Gargantua qu'il instituast sa religion au contraire de toutes aultres. (*Gargantua,* LII)

The monk then requested Gargantua to institute his religious order in an exactly contrary way to all others.

1. There are no walls.
2. There is no clock:

> selon les occasions et opportunitéz seroient toutes les oeuvres dispensées . . . la plus grande resverie du monde estoit soy gouverner au son d'une cloche, et non au dicté de bon sens et entendement. (Ibid.)

affairs should be conducted according to chance and opportunity. . . . the greatest nonsense in the world was to regulate one's life by the sound of a bell, instead of by the promptings of reason and good sense.

3. There is no separation of the sexes. Both men and women are admitted (but only attractive men and beautiful women, 'bien formés et bien naturés'), and are encouraged to enjoy each other's company. Marriage is allowed:

> là honorablement on peult estre marié. (Ibid.)

anyone could be regularly married.

4. The women dress according to the season, and to the current fashion. The finest clothes and jewellery are to be worn.
5. Having once entered Thélème, nobody is obliged to spend the rest of his life there. He can change his mind and leave when he likes:

THE NATURALISM OF RABELAIS

> feust estably que tant hommes que femmes là repceuz sortiroient quand bon leur sembleroit, franchement et entièrement. (Ibid.)
>
> it was decreed that both men and women, once accepted, could depart from there whenever they pleased, without let or hindrance.

6. Riches and comfort are not despised. The monastery is to compete with the finest Renaissance palaces.

7. Most important of all, the only rule is not to have any:

> Toute leur vie estoit employée non par loix, statuz ou reigles, mais selon leur vouloir et franc arbitre.
>
> All their life was regulated not by laws, statutes, or rules, but according to their free will and pleasure.

They get up when they feel like it, retire when they want to, work when and only when the desire impels them. No authority forces them to do anything against their wishes. The only rule which Gargantua establishes is the straightforward:

> FAY CE QUE VOULDRAS
>
> DO WHAT YOU WILL.

for the moment you create rules and prohibitions, you create the desire to break them:

> car nous entreprenons tousjours choses défendues et convoitons ce que nous est dénié. (*Gargantua*, LVII)
>
> For we always strive after things forbidden and covet what is denied us.

8. Learning is an essential part of Thelemite life. All inhabitants can sing, read, write, play musical instruments, speak five or six languages.

The abbey is not open to everyone. Unlike More's *Utopia*, Thélème is designed for a select aristocracy, both by class and intellect. The following are welcomed.

> tous nobles chevaliers, tous gentilz compaignons, Évangélicques, dames de hault paraige.
> (*Gargantua*, LIV)

> noble gentlemen ... good companions ... Evangelists ... ladies of high lineage

while the door is closed to hypocrites, bigots, lawyers, usurers, and people with the pox.

Of course, the worship of God is also on the agenda (*pace* Lefranc), but it is an individual kind of worship, not collective. No vows are pronounced. Life is to be enjoyed to the full, with elegant and intelligent conversation, sport, the arts, all that contributes to the shaping of a cultured Renaissance man. Thélème resembles more a literary rest-home than an institution.

It is perhaps unnecessary to point out that the Abbaye de Thélème represents the dream of a progressive Humanist. It is the expression of an ideal, not the blue-print of a plan. Because it is purely imaginary (and unrealizable), Rabelais's description of Thelemite life is exaggerated, if only to show, by contrast, the faults inherent in the existing monastical system.

C. Filial Duty

The responsibility and good-feeling of a son towards his father are also part of human nature, and much praised by Rabelais. Gargantua and Pantagruel have an extremely strong and affectionate personal relationship. They write to each other regularly, consult each other in important matters; Gargantua is always offering friendly advice, and Pantagruel always accepting it. The father signs one letter as 'Ton père et amy,

THE NATURALISM OF RABELAIS

Gargantua'. This same letter (*Quart Livre*, III) begs Pantagruel to write more often and dissipate the father's fears for his son's safety at sea:

> Filz très cher, l'affection que naturellement porte le père à son filz bien aymé est en mon endroict tant accreue... que, depuis ton partement, me a, non une foys, tollu tout aultre pensement, me délaissant on cueur ceste unicque et soigneuse paour que vostre embarquement ayt esté de quelque meschaing ou fascherie accompaigné.

> My dearest son, The natural affection which a father feels for his beloved son is so much increased in my case... that, since your departure it has more than once driven every other thought from my mind. Only one care and fear has remained with me, that some misfortune or difficulty may have followed your embarkation.

There is a justly famous speech by Pantagruel in which he promises not to marry without his father's permission and approval. He is impelled not so much by an abstract 'duty' as by a natural wish to please:

> Plus tost prie Dieu estre à voz piedz veu roydde mort en vostre desplaisir que sans vostre plaisir estre veu vif marié.
> (*Tiers Livre*, XLVIII)

> I would rather lie stark dead at your feet and under your displeasure than be found living and married without your consent.

The ties of love which unite father and son, arising spontaneously from their nature, and not imposed by parental authority, constitute one of the most moving elements in Rabelais's books. And the various letters which give expression to this love are, incidentally, among the most elegant pieces of prose in the entire work.

8

On Aggression

Rabelais is a pacifist who detests violence, injustice and oppression. War is the greatest of all evils, because it brings suffering to innocent people. Rabelais thinks that every avenue must be explored in an effort to avoid war – negotiation, Christian good-will, flattery, deterrence – and if all else fails, and fighting becomes necessary, then a defensive war is the only kind he will allow in a civilized society. His greatest anger is reserved for wars of conquest or pride.

Rabelais's political ideas, or at least his views on war and aggression, find their highest expression in the chapters on the Picrocholine War in *Gargantua*. The story is briefly this: The farming people of Grandgousier's country are tending their vineyard one fine Spring day, when some bakers from Lerné pass with wagon-loads of fresh cakes, on their way to Chinon. The farmers, very partial to these cakes, ask if they may buy some, but the bakers simply hurl abuse at them. One of the farmers, Forgier, protests that this is not the way to behave, whereupon the baker Marquet calls him over, promising to give one of his cakes. In his innocence, Forgier believes him, approaches, and receives a powerful blow across the legs. He responds by striking Marquet across the head and pulling him from his mare. The farmers take as many cakes as they want, paying the proper amount for them all, and send the irascible bakers packing.

The bakers complain to their king, Picrochole, who, without pausing to think, launches a bloody war of aggression on the people of Grandgousier. The latter goes to war with a heavy heart; he fights reluctantly, but with determination, and is finally victorious. Thus ends the 'grand débat dont furent faictes grosses guerres'.

The story is very vividly told, with particularly realistic scenes of carnage and bloodshed. But there is another kind of realism in this story, an historical realism. The whole episode is said to be an allegory of the struggle between François 1er and Charles V, with Grandgousier as Louis XII, Gargantua as François 1er, Pantagruel as Henri II, and Picrochole as Charles-Quint. All this is quite possible. Though a pacifist, Rabelais was also a Frenchman and a patriot, who supported the king and was frequently called upon to act as royal propagandist.

Even more precisely, recent research has demonstrated that the whole conflict is based on a true story in which Rabelais's father, Antoine, played a leading role. Records show that there was a territorial dispute between Antoine Rabelais and his neighbour, Gaucher de Sainte-Marthe, based on a silly quarrel about a river. Accordingly, Grandgousier is Antoine Rabelais, and Picrochole is Gaucher de Sainte-Marthe. The story is all the more convincing when one realizes that Gaucher de Sainte-Marthe was in fact Seigneur de Lerné, 'tiers de ce nom' like Picrochole, that Antoine Rabelais did have a relation and friend called Jehan Gallet, a lawyer like himself, who negotiated in the dispute (in the Picrocholine War he is called Ulrich Gallet), and that all the place names correspond to actual places around Rabelais's birthplace, La Devinière, which are still on the map of France today. It is also interesting that one of the fiercest attacks against Rabelais, some years later, came from Charles de Sainte-Marthe, son of Gaucher. It can have been no secret to his contemporaries that Charles was revenging himself for the libel on his father in the account of the Picrocholine War.

All of the above knowledge we owe to Abel Lefranc and his team, whose indefatigable researches have done more than

A. The Immorality of War

Grandgousier is extremely reluctant to go to war, preferring to negotiate with his adversary:

> Je n'entreprendray guerre que je n'aye essayé tous les ars et moyens de paix; là je me résouls.
> (*Gargantua*, XXVIII)

> I will not embark upon war till I have tried every art and means of peace. On that I am resolved.

But, if necessary, he is prepared to defend his lands, since he owes a responsibility to protect his subjects:

> La raison le veult ainsi, car de leur labeur je suis entretenu et de leur sueur je suis nourry, moy, mes enfans et ma famille.
> (Ibid.)

> Justice demands it. For by their labour I am supported, by their sweat I am fed, I and my wife and family.

He will initially seek to obviate war by persuasion, having been all his life a man of peace:

> Ma délibération n'est de provocquer, ains de apaiser; d'assaillir, mais défendre; de conquester, mais de guarder mes féaulx subjectz et terres héréditaires.
> (*Gargantua*, XXIX)

> My intention is not to provoke, but to appease; not to attack, but to defend; not to conquer, but to guard my loyal subjects and hereditary lands.

ON AGGRESSION

However, if fighting cannot be avoided,

> L'exploict sera faict à moindre effusion de sang que sera possible. (Ibid.)

Our measures will be carried out with the least possible bloodshed.

As a last resort, a final attempt to appease, Grandgousier sends his envoy Gallet to plead reason with Picrochole. Gallet's diplomacy appeals to the king's common sense, to his compassion, and adds a little subtle flattery. He tells Picrochole that:

> La chose est tant hors les metes de raison, tant abhorrente de sens commun, que à peine peut elle estre par humain entendement conceue. (*Gargantua,* XXXI)

This thing is far beyond the bounds of reason, so repugnant to common sense, as to be scarcely conceivable to human understanding.

and reprimands him gently for having made no attempt to discover the truth of the offence before declaring war:

> tu debvois premier enquérir de la vérité, puis nous en admonester. (Ibid.)

you should first have inquired into the truth of the matter and then have given us warning.

Conciliation fails to assuage the evil temper of Picrochole, who, urged and prodded by his advisers, now has dreams of conquering the whole world. (The scene in which Picrochole's greed for power is fed by his unscrupulous counsellors is one of the funniest in the book.) Grandgousier returns the cakes, but it is too late; battle is joined.

A final word on the immorality of war from Grandgousier, talking to his prisoner Toucquedillon:

Le temps n'est plus d'ainsi conquester les royaulmes avecques dommaige de son prochain frère christian. Ceste imitation des anciens Hercules, Alexandres, Hannibalz, Scipions, Césars et aultres telz, est contraire à la profession de l'Évangile, par lequel nous est commandé guarder, saulver, régir et administrer chascun ses pays et terres, non hostilement envahir les aultres, et, ce que les Sarazins et Barbares jadis appelloient prouesses, maintenant nous appellons briguanderies et méchancetéz.... Si guerre la nommez, elle n'est que superficiaire, elle n'entre poinct au profond cabinet de noz cueurs: car nul de nous n'est oultraigé en son honneur.

(*Gargantua,* XLVI)

The time is past for the conquering of kingdoms, to the hurt of his Christian neighbour and brother. This emulation of the ancient Herculeses, Alexanders, Hannibals, Scipios, Caesars, and suchlike, is contrary to Gospel teaching, by which we are enjoined each to guard, protect, rule and administer his own lands and territories, and not to make hostile attacks on those of others. What the Saracens and Barbarians of old called deeds of prowess we now call robbery and wickedness. . . . However, if you do call it war, it is only skin-deep; it has not entered into the secret places of our hearts. For none of us has been wronged in his honour.

One should notice the speed with which Grandgousier's army is mobilized, once the order has been given. Pacifist or not, he believes in being prepared, and values the deterrent effect of a large stock-pile of arms and a well-trained fighting force. He is also a subtle psychologist in matters of military strategy:

selon vraye discipline militaire, jamais ne fault mettre son ennemy en lieu de désespoir, parce que telle nécessité luy multiplie sa force et accroist le couraige. . . . Ouvrez tousjours à voz ennemys toutes les portes et chemins, et plustost leurs faictes un pont d'argent affin de les renvoyer.

(*Gargantua,* XLIII)

according to true military practice you must never drive your enemy into the straits of despair, because such a plight multiplies his strength and increases his courage . . . Always leave every door and road open to your enemies. Make them a bridge of silver, in fact, to help them get away.

B. Magnanimity in Victory

Once success has been achieved, Rabelais's heroes make no attempt to bring the vanquished enemy to his knees. They seek neither to humiliate nor to destroy him. There are no victory celebrations, no triumphal marches, no severe punishments visited on the sorry soldiers who have lost. On the contrary, Grandgousier's treatment of the defeated foe is humane in every respect. Far from pillaging their land and ransacking their homes, he gives them money and food enough to help them re-establish their economy, and retains for just punishment only the handful of men responsible for having started the hostilities. The rest receive nothing worse than a lecture from their victor Gargantua:

> maintenant je vous absoluz et délivre, et vous rends francs et libères comme par avant. D'abondant, serez à l'yssue des portes payéz, chascun pour troys moys, pour vous pouvoir retirer en voz maisons et familles, et vous conduiront en saulveté six cens hommes d'armes et huyct mille hommes de pied, soubz la conduite de mon escuyer Alexandre, affin que par les paisans ne soyez oultragéz. Dieu soit avecques vous.   (*Gargantua*, L)

I now absolve and deliver you, and make you as free and independent as before. Moreover, as you go out through the gate every one of you shall be given three months' pay, so that you may return to your homes and families; and you shall be safely escorted by six hundred men-at-arms and eight thousand foot under the command of my squire Alexander, so that you shall not be molested by the peasants. God be with you.

His generosity extends even to Picrochole's five-year-old son, providing for the boy's education and comfort, and promising to surrender to him, on his majority, the lands which he has just conquered, and which are the child's by rightful inheritance.

The abbey of Thélème may have been a pure construction of Rabelais's imagination, impossible of realization. But the magnanimity shown by the giants in victory was no idealistic chimera; it was based on fact, on the policies of the king, and especially those of the Humanist men of war. One of Rabelais's protectors, du Bellay, Seigneur de Langey (whose death Rabelais laments so eloquently in the *Quart Livre*), was just such a man. Langey forbade his soldiers to take anything from the conquered people of Piémont without paying for it, and he himself spent a large part of his personal fortune making good the damage done to enemy lands in war. He bought food for the starving population. The giants' humanity was therefore not only possible, but found a parallel in reality. The first chapter of the *Tiers Livre* is devoted to an expression of this humanity which Abel Lefranc has called 'le plus beau manifeste d'humanité que le XVIe siècle ait fait entendre'. In it, Pantagruel says that the victor's duty is to promote the well-being of the vanquished, for practical as well as moral reasons:

> la manière d'entretenir et retenir pays nouvellement conquestéz n'est ... les peuples pillant, forçant, angariant, ruinant, mal vexant et régissant avecques verges de fer .... Comme enfant nouvellement né les fault alaicter, bercer, esjouir. Comme arbre nouvellement planté les fault appuyer, asceurer, défendre de toutes vimères, injures et calamitez. Comme personne saulvé de longue et forte maladie et venant à convalescence les fault choyer, espargner, restaurer.

> the way of preserving and retaining newly conquered countries is not to pillage, distress, torment, ruin, and persecute the people, ruling them with a rod of iron. ... Newly conquered peoples have

to be suckled, cradled and dandled, like new-born children. Like freshly planted trees they have to be propped, supported and protected from all disasters, damage and calamities. Like men recovering from a long and severe illness and returning to convalescence, they must be indulged, pampered, and restored to life.

Finally, to return once more to the Picrocholine War, Gargantua says that he has no intention of erecting a useless monument to commemorate the war, preferring that his magnanimity towards the vanquished should provide sufficient memorial. My ancestors have always, he says,

> pour signe mémorial des triumphes et victoires, plus voluntiers érigé trophées et monumens ès cueurs des vaincuz par grâce que, ès terres par eulx conquestées, par architecture.
> *(Gargantua,* L)

have preferred to erect monuments in the hearts of the vanquished by a display of clemency, than to raise trophies in the form of architecture in the lands they have conquered.

C. Rabelais's Political Ideal

Rabelais's ideal is startlingly simple: peace, prosperity and justice under the benign rule of a cultured and intelligent monarch. There is not the slightest hint of revolution in his writings. It appears not to have occurred to him to wish for any other rule than that of a patriarchal monarchy. As Erasmus did before him, and Voltaire was to do much later, Rabelais admires the famous quotation from Plato's *Republic*, to which Gargantua makes reference in his speech to the pilgrims:

> lors les républiques seroient heureuses quand les roys philosopheroient ou les philosophes régneroient.
> *(Gargantua,* XLV)

states will only be happy when the kings shall be philosophers and the philosophers kings.

D. Royal Propagandist

Rabelais admired François 1er for his culture and humanity. He was, perhaps, fairly close to the ideal of a philosopher-king. It was François 1er who had founded the 'lecteurs royaux' in 1530, dedicated to the teaching of Greek and Hebrew, and again François who gave the weight of his support to Rabelais by granting a royal licence for the publication of his works in 1545. In short, François 1er was the ideal Humanist monarch.

One must also bear in mind that Rabelais was a fervent patriot. He knew and loved his country well. He even represented France abroad in a semi-official capacity, and held political posts towards the end of his life (see Chapter 1).

It therefore comes as no surprise to discover that Rabelais often writes as unofficial spokesman for the king. When he talks of his giants' attitude towards conquered peoples, he is not merely philosophizing, but publicizing French foreign policy. When he unleashes his satirical talent against the Pope in the *Quart Livre*, he is supporting the official attitude of the French government. When he allows Pantagruel to attack young people who marry without their parents' consent, he is not only expressing the filial affection of his hero, but again supporting the king, who had taken measures to prevent clandestine marriages. In the *Almanach pour l'an 1535*, Rabelais says that France is happier, more prosperous and more peaceful than it has been for fifty years, and should there linger any further doubt, the magnificent Prologue to the *Tiers Livre* reads like a superb patriotic hymn.

9

The Medieval Legacy

The whole of this essay so far has been concerned with Rabelais the Renaissance man and Humanist. But there is more to him than that, as those who have never even read him are aware. In common with most of his contemporaries, Rabelais straddles the transitional period between Middle Ages and Renaissance so well that his books contain elements of both. Indeed, it is not unusual to find Renaissance elegance and medieval coarseness overlapping on the same page. Both in style and content, Rabelais belongs as much to the past as he does to the future, and it is right that we should examine in what ways he remains medieval. They can be resumed as follows:

1. A lack of order or arrangement. One has the impression that he has thrown all his ideas on to the paper as they occurred to him. This is a lack of what the French call 'le goût'.

2. A taste for vulgarity, coarse humour, obscene jokes.

3. His dismissive treatment of women, and his reducing heterosexual love to the level of sexual gratification.

4. His style sometimes shows a medieval leaning towards argumentation and the easy paradox.

5. His pedantry, the indulgent display of his immense knowledge.

6. The realism and detail of his topographical descriptions.

7. The gratuitous cruelty in his accounts of carnage and slaughter.

8. His predilection for tedious enumerations, plays on words, antistrophes, puns, etc.

9. Finally, his subject itself – the childhood and adventures of a fabulous giant – is taken from medieval folklore.

A. Le Gros Rire

> Mieulx est de ris que de larmes escripre. Pour ce que rire est le propre de l'homme.
>
> (*Gargantua,* 'Aux lecteurs')

Mirth's my theme and tears are not, For laughter is man's proper lot.

Examples of coarse humour abound. The number of codpieces, cocks, and arse-holes mentioned in the five books must add up to some hundreds. We are told that Gargantua's name derives from the first words his father was heard to utter when he saw the child – Que grand tu as! (What a big one you've got!) As an infant, Gargantua amuses himself by aiming his piss against the sun. He shat at every hour, 'car il estoit merveilleusement phlegmaticque des fesses'. Frère Jean explains that he has a long nose because 'ma nourrice avoit les tetins moletz' (my wet-nurse had soft tits).

Sometimes the joke is sustained for an entire chapter, as when Panurge falls in love with an aristocratic lady from Paris. His opening gambit when he approaches her is not the most delicate:

> Madame, saichez que je suis tant amoureux de vous que je n'en peuz ny pisser ny fianter!   (*Pantagruel,* XXI)

Madame, I must tell you that I am so amorous of you that I can neither piss nor shit for love.

Getting nowhere with the fine lady, Panurge plays a trick on her, by sprinkling over her expensive garments a special drug he has mixed, whose property is to attract dogs. Immediately, all the dogs in the church trot towards her, and,

THE MEDIEVAL LEGACY

> Petitz et grands, gros et menuz, tous y venoyent, tirans le
> membre, et la sentens, et pissant partout sur elle.
>
> (*Pantagruel*, XXII)
>
> Small and great, big and little, all came, lifting their legs, smelling
> her, and pissing all over her.

Before long, she is covered in urine from head to foot, and Panurge, prostrate with laughter, makes the comment that she must be on heat.

Pantagruel's explanation of how to wipe one's arse with the neck of a goose, already mentioned for its satirical intention in an earlier chapter, none the less has obvious salacious attractions.

Passages such as these are written with an enviable talent for provoking laughter by treating the absurd seriously. Rabelais seems to have his tongue permanently in his cheek. This, it must be admitted, is the talent which has maintained his popularity untarnished for 400 years. Indeed, in the nineteenth century, Rabelais was valued *only* for his coarse humour. Émile Faguet wrote, with a haughty condescension which now seems incredible, that Rabelais had an 'elementary' wit, an 'esprit de village français, qui ne manque pas de saveur du reste pour les lecteurs au-dessous de douze ans'. While in England, on the other hand, Rabelais's book was kept on the top shelf, out of the reach of impressionable children, only lifted down to amuse the gentlemen over port while the ladies were in the withdrawing-room. One manual of French literature dating from 1872 is remarkably prim, but not unique, when it says that 'the disgusting coarseness of his style must ever make his work a sealed book for the majority of readers'.[1]

B. Le Fabuleux

Much comic effect is obtained from the sheer size of the heroes, when describing how many thousands of yards of material are

[1] Gustave Masson, *Clan Book of French Literature* (Edinburgh).

needed to make their clothes, or the amount of food required to nourish them. Rabelais was called by one critic 'L'Homère de la mangeaille' as a result. Even now, it is the fantastic amount of food consumed which has remained the signature of Rabelais in popular taste. Hence we refer to a 'Gargantuan' meal. Similarly, the comic effect of 'How Pantagruel covered a whole army with his tongue' or 'How Gargantua ate six pilgrims in his salad' lies exclusively in the gigantic proportions of the heroes. To be fair, however, Rabelais more often than not forgets the size of his heroes. Their strictly 'fabulous' exploits occupy a relatively small place in the narrative. The *Tiers Livre*, for instance, does not mention that Pantagruel is a giant.

C. Puns, Enumerations, Inventions, etc.

Weights, measures, and numbers are detailed with absurd precision. When, in Chapter XVII of *Gargantua*, the giant undoes his codpiece, waves his cock in the air, and pisses on the population of Paris, he drowns two hundred and sixty thousand, four hundred and eighteen people, not counting the women and children. In Chapter XXII, the list of games which Gargantua plays occupies several pages. The number of casualties in the Picrocholine War is stated with minute precision. Such ridiculous exactness was a much-used comic effect in the Middle Ages.

So were the puns. Never mind about the 'service divin', says Frère Jean, what about the 'service du vin'. Paris was so named because its inhabitants had been drowned 'par rys'. And so on. Chapter V of *Gargantua* – Les Propos des Bien Yvres – is packed with puns.

Rabelais often uses the 'antistrophe', or purposeful malapropism. He mixes up 'femme folle à la messe' with 'femme molle à la fesse'. The wounded Épistémon does not have 'la tête coupée', but 'la couppe testée'.

On occasion, Rabelais is not averse to inventing words, piling a list of verbs one after the other to make the action he is describing more vivid, more picturesque. He is a master at draining every possible comic effect from a word. The scores of proper nouns and names he invents are amusing even in isolation (Merdaille, Tournemoule, Basdefesses, Trepelu, etc.). No French writer has ever exploited the comic power of words as much or as successfully as Rabelais. Lanson has said that only Victor Hugo surpassed him in his appreciation of 'la joie du mot'. Pierre Villey talks of his 'ivresse lexicographique'. Abel Lefranc states categorically that Rabelais is 'le plus grand virtuose qui ait jamais existé dans notre langue'. Certainly, the richness, expressive power, and extent of Rabelais's vocabulary are astonishing. There seems to be no local slang with which he is not acquainted, no archaic word whose precise meaning he does not know. There is no doubt that his work is a dictionary in itself, offering philological historians an extremely valuable record of the written and spoken language of the sixteenth century.

One critic has suggested that Rabelais treats words as matter. Just as the painter uses colours to represent an object, so Rabelais uses sounds. 'Une sorte d'assomption de la matière s'accomplit chez Rabelais lorsqu'il a compris qu'on peut parler avec des sons, suggérer un sens à partir de la chair des mots. Il faudra attendre Hugo, Joyce, Valéry pour retrouver cela. Le passage de la forme au fond se fera par contamination verbale, suggestion contenue: des mots exploratoires créeront l'atmosphère, mettront un halo psychologique autour de l'objet . . .'[1]

D. Erudition and Pedantry

Rabelais belongs to the Middle Ages by the pedantic display of his staggering knowledge. There are thousands of quotations from Greek and Latin writers, nearly always *à propos*, but often

[1] Manuel de Diéguez, *Rabelais par lui-même*.

unnecessary. Not content to tell us that Gargamelle's pregnancy lasted eleven months, he quotes parallels from various sources. The 'propos torcheculatif' is supported by copious references, specifying chapter and line of his source material. His literary authority is trumpeted before us, as if to impress. He shows us that he has studied legal history (e.g. the Bridoye episode). The *Tiers Livre* has been called the most erudite book of the century, demonstrating the widest possible knowledge of all branches of learning. Rabelais's medical studies are likewise tapped for reference material. He shows an intimate knowledge of anatomy when he describes the route taken by Gargantua through his mother's body to exit through her left ear, when he describes the slaughter of war ('Frère Jean deslochoit les spondyles du coul,' etc.), and when he justifies the attention given to hygiene and health in Gargantua's pedagogic programme. There are countless other examples one could mention.

More importantly, Rabelais's style often shows evidence of medieval pedantry. We have already mentioned the opening chapters of the *Tiers Livre*, in which Panurge defends his need to borrow money in a tedious argument, typical of medieval hair-splitting scholastics. One other example will serve to illustrate the point:

> Je interprète (dist Pantagruel) avoir et n'avoir femme en ceste facon: que femme avoir est l'avoir à l'usaige tel que Nature la créa, qui est pour l'ayde, esbatement et société de l'homme; n'avoir femme est ne soy apoiltronner autour d'elle, pour elle ne contaminer celle unicque et suprême affection que doibt l'homme à Dieu; ne laisser les offices qu'il doibt naturellement à sa patrie, à la République, à ses amys; ne mettre en non chaloir ses estudes et négoces, pour continuellement à sa femme complaire. Prenant en ceste manière avoir et n'avoir femme, je ne voids répugnance ne contradiction ès termes.
>
> (*Tiers Livre*, XXXV)

> I interpret having and not having a wife in this way, said Pantagruel, that to have a wife is to have her for the purpose for which Nature created her, that is for the aid, pleasure, and society of man. Not to have her means not to be tied to her apron-strings; not for her sake to debase the unique and supreme love that man owes to God; not to neglect the duties that man owes to his country, the community, and his friends; not to abandon his studies and his business in order to be continuously waiting on his wife. Taking having and not having a wife in this way I see no conflict or contradiction in terms.

It is no accident that this passage is bewildering, whereas most of Rabelais is sparklingly clear. It is because the style is incontestably medieval in pomposity and wilful obscurity. There is the world of difference between a passage like this, and the sharp clarity and classical elegance of, for example, Gargantua's letter to Pantagruel, or his address to the defeated army of Picrochole. In Rabelais, the polished Ciceronian prose and the clumsy medieval rhetoric exist side by side.

E. On Women

The world inhabited by Gargantua and Pantagruel is overwhelmingly masculine. Women are hardly mentioned in the first two books, except in the chapters on the abbey of Thélème, to which they are admitted (*a*) for their decorative value, (*b*) to give pleasure to the men, and (*c*) because they were not normally allowed in a monastery. The habit of masculine predominance which permeates these books is distinctly medieval in origin. The Renaissance was later to appreciate the finer qualities of the fair sex, their elegance, charm, and delicacy. Rabelais, however, remained staunchly anti-feminist, not to say misogynistic, when he eventually discussed the subject in his *Tiers Livre*.

Panurge consults a variety of authorities to discover whether or not he should marry. A poet, a magician, a theologian, a doctor, a philosopher, a lawyer, all warn him, in one way or another, that women are deceitful, stupid, unreliable. They deflect men from their studies, from their duty to country, from their attention to friends. The doctor Rondibilis is the most eloquent in his contempt:

> Quand je diz femme, je diz un sexe tant fragil, tant variable, tant muable, tant inconstant et imperfeict, que Nature me semble s'estre esguarée de ce bon sens par lequel elle avoit créé et formé toutes choses, quand elle a basty la femme... forgeant la femme, elle a eu esguard à la sociale délectation de l'homme et à la perpétuité de l'espèce humaine.... Certes Platon ne sçait en quel ranc il les doibve colloquer, ou des animaux raisonnables, ou des bestes brutes. (*Tiers Livre*, XXXII)

> When I say women, I speak of a sex so frail, so variable, so easily moved, so inconstant and imperfect that, in constructing woman, Nature seems to me to have lapsed badly from the intelligence she showed in the creation and shaping of all other things... when she shaped woman she had far more thought for the social delectation of man and the perpetuation of the human race... Plato does not know in what way to class them, whether as reasoning animals or brute beasts.

The only kind of wife worth considering is she who passively and unquestioningly submits to her husband's will in every respect,

> 'celle qui plus s'efforce avecques Dieu soy former en bonne grâce et conformer aux meurs de son mary.'
> (*Tiers Livre*, XXX)

> one who with God's help strives hardest to keep herself in good grace and to conform to her husband's way of life.

In all this, Rabelais is faithful to the contemporary scholastic tradition of contemptuous dismissal of the female sex, and to the medieval conviction that women were naturally inferior beings. It is men alone who take part in the discussion, calmly theorizing on the merits or otherwise of women as if they were a metaphysical abstraction. No woman is invited to give her view. She is only useful in so far as she plays her part in marriage.

Rabelais's misogyny is not entirely representative of his age. There were those who thought otherwise. Indeed, as Abel Lefranc has again shown, the subject had been fiercely argued for some twenty years before the *Tiers Livre* was published. Rabelais was saying his word in a controversy which was on everyone's lips. Erasmus had written his *Institution du Mariage Chrétien* in 1526, in which he had said that 'La femme est un animal inepte et ridicule . . . La femme est toujours femme, c'est-à-dire stupide'. Cornelius Agrippa (the model for Rabelais's Her Trippa) had published a *De praecellentia foeminei sexus* in 1529, and Gratien Dupont a *Controverses des sexe masculin et foeminin* in 1534. The most famous treatise of the period was Antoine Héroet's *La Parfaicte Amye*, which was pro-feminist, and to which Rabelais's *Tiers Livre* may very well have been an answer. Lefranc quotes at length from François de Billon's contemporary account of the quarrel, in which Rabelais is cited as one of the leaders of the anti-feminist movement.

In his book, *The Rabelaisian Marriage*, M. A. Screech advanced an entirely new interpretation of Rabelais's attitude towards women, at variance with the foregoing comments. Screech entirely rejects Lefranc's conclusion that Rabelais was on the side of the anti-feminists. 'Rabelais the anti-feminist extremist never existed,' he writes. 'Rabelais intends to show, in the teeth of traditional arguments in favour of celibacy, that matrimony, as befits the greatest of God's earthly gifts, is a potential good. He praises marriage in the clearest terms – yet he also reminds us through the death of Badebec that marriage relationships must be treated with indifference.'

Screech points out that the advice offered by the doctor

Rondibilis contains a cool scientific assessment of the nature of womankind, and in particular the nature of the womb, which is considered as an independent being in its own right, difficult to control. Hence the treatment of woman as an 'animal' has been misunderstood. Rabelais does not wish to show contempt for the female sex by the use of such terms, but merely to state a scientific fact, devoid of emotional overtones, a fact with which marriage partners must come to terms.

In the great debate on the value of women, Rabelais adopts a middle course, praising legitimate marriage as an honourable state which can be a source of happiness, but warning that it is fraught with problems.

Screech's researches into this aspect of Rabelais's thought are highly stimulating and important. But it remains true that, though matrimony be advocated as a desirable state, women enter into the picture only in so far as they are a necessary partner. They are scarcely held in high regard for their own sakes; it is the relationship of father to son that tends to excite Rabelais's enthusiasm rather than that of husband to wife.

F. Realism

We have already seen that the scenario of the Picrocholine War is exactly and precisely situated in the area around Rabelais's birthplace at La Devinière. The topographical details make it possible to follow the course of the war on a map. Similarly, the voyage of Pantagruel and Panurge in the *Quart Livre*, though coloured by fantasy, is geographically accurate, being based in some measure on the travels of Jacques Cartier. The description of the Abbey of Thélème provides a vivid and accurate picture of Renaissance architecture and costumes (and, moreover, had it really existed it would be situated at the confluence of the Indre and the Loire). The accounts of student life and lawyers' circles are likewise based on closely observed reality. Finally, many of the characters in the story may be drawn from life, being based on people whom Rabelais knew; Grandgousier is his father Antoine Rabelais, Rondibilis is a doctor whom he knew in Montpellier, Hippothadée is Lefèvre d'Étaples, Raminagrobis is Jean le Maire de Belges.[1] Further research may one day reveal the sources of Rabelais's entire gallery of characters:

Je ne bâtis que pierres vives: ce sont hommes.

[1] See Lefranc, op. cit., pp. 127, etc.

10
Some Portraits and Opinions

1. Grandgousier

The eldest of the giants is a grave, serious, responsible man. He is conscious of his duty towards the people who depend upon him for their livelihood. On one level, this is the king responsible to his subjects, on another, the landowner (Antoine Rabelais?) responsible to his peasants. He has a high moral concept of honour and justice, which he displays in his treatment of the conquered enemy. He is sensible, intelligent, well-educated, a practical philosopher who is concerned with acting for the best happiness of all. Grandgousier's roots are in the country; he retains the peasant's love of the earth, his capacity for simple amusement. He is also patient, tactful, diplomatic. He is personally hurt and offended that his friend Picrochole should take up arms against him, and at first refuses to believe such a thing possible. He is profoundly religious, loyal to his family, a peaceful man who wants nothing better than to live at home, in the affection of wife and son, at peace with the world:

> Las! ma vieillesse ne requerroit dorénavant que repous, et toute ma vie n'ay rien tant procuré que paix.
>
> (*Gargantua*, XXVIII)

Alas, all that my old age called for was repose. All my life I have sought peace above all things.

2. Gargantua

Grandgousier's son is at first a petulant and stupid child who bursts into tears when asked a question to which he does not

SOME PORTRAITS AND OPINIONS 99

immediately know the answer. Shy and timid with strangers, he shows no promise of growing into anything but a bawdy hedonist (except of course for the childish antics which owe their fun to his gigantic status). After the Humanist tutor Ponocrates takes him under his wing, Gargantua changes. He becomes the ideal Renaissance prince, knowledgeable in every sphere, adept at all things, an articulate and persuasive orator, fine general, and subtle politician. By the end of the book, Gargantua has become wise and prudent, a fitting heir to his father's estates and responsibilities.

3. Pantagruel

Son to Gargantua and grandson to Grandgousier, Pantagruel inherits the family's disproportionate size. He has the additional power of provoking thirst in all whom he meets. But these fabulous details soon lose their relevance in the course of the story. In his youth, his only ambition is to have a good time, to enjoy himself in the company of amusing friends and indulge in those riotous escapades of which students have always been capable. But he too, like Shakespeare's Prince Hal, matures into a responsible citizen. More, he becomes the embodiment of benign morality, of which his affectionate protectiveness towards Panurge is a fine illustration. Pantagruel gradually acquires the wisdom and sense of responsibility of his forefathers, growing into a man of good sense and moderation. He is altogether a thoroughly likeable chap, loyal, warm-hearted, and loath to think ill of anyone:

> C'estoit le meilleur petit et grand bon hommet qui oncques ceigneit espée. Toutes choses prenoit en bonne partie, tout acte interprétoit à bien. Jamais ne se tourmentoit, jamais ne se scandalizoit. (*Tiers, Livre*, II)

he was the best little great good fellow that ever wore a sword. He took everything in good part, put favourable interpretation on every act, never tormented himself, and was never scandalized.

4. Panurge

We meet Panurge for the first time in Chapter IX of *Pantagruel*, 'Comment Pantagruel trouva Panurge, lequel il ayma toute sa vie.' He is described as:

> un homme beau de stature et élégant en tous linéamens du corps, mais pitoyablement navré en divers lieux et tant mal en ordre qu'il semblait estre eschappé ès chiens.

> a man of handsome build, elegant in all his features, but pitifully wounded in various places, and in so sorry a state that he looked as if he had escaped from the dogs.

Later, we are told that he is about thirty-five years old, a bit of a lecher, and naturally subject to an illness called 'faulte d'argent'. But he has sixty-three different ways of getting money when he needs it, of which the most honourable and most common is theft, 'façon de larrecin furtivement faict'. He is a rogue, a cheat, a vagabond, a boozer, a roysterer, but otherwise 'le meilleur filz du monde'.

Pantagruel and Panurge form an immediate bond of friendship characterized by affectionate loyalty on both sides. Panurge serves his master best by the cunning invention of his wit. There are a thousand little tricks which his fertile and agile mind can perform, some teasingly malicious. Panurge is an active man, happy only when he is doing something. His intelligence is limited, but his inventiveness knows no bounds. His idea of justice is elementary, but basically sound:

> Jamais homme ne me feist plaisir sans récompense, ou recongnoissance pour le moins. Je ne suys pas ingrat, et ne le feuz, ne seray. Jamais homme ne me feist desplaisir sans repentance, ou en ce monde, ou en l'aultre. Je ne suis poinct fat jusques là.   (*Quart Livre*, VIII)

> No man ever did me a good turn without getting a reward, or at least an acknowledgement. I'm not an ungrateful man, I never was and never will be. And nobody's ever done me a bad turn without being sorry for it, either in this world or the next. I'm not such a fool as that.

Another way in which Panurge can serve Pantagruel is by inspiring courage and fortitude in Pantagruel's army. He is himself brave to a fault, ready to die for his master, encourages and comforts his companions, is ever ready at Pantagruel's side in time of danger.

Thus far at least, Panurge represents a type common enough in literary tradition, that of the cunning, cheeky servant who provides an effective contrast with the noble, high-minded hero, and who is the incarnation of subtle strategy and farcical tricks.

Panurge, however, changes character rather drastically from the *Tiers Livre* onwards. From being the soul of courage, he becomes a meek and weak-kneed coward, afraid at the slightest shadow of danger. His insolence, bad temper, self-regarding prudence all increase to the detriment of his loyalty to Pantagruel. As the latter says, 'L'esprit malin vous séduit.' M. A. Screech has described him thus: 'With Pantagruel all is firm, wise, calm, decided. As soon as we leave him for Panurge, we leave wisdom and find stupidity; calmness and find agitation; decision and find all that is hesitant and sporadic. For with Panurge nothing is settled and nothing is final. He reaches a decision only to abandon it; his fatal fluency of argument serves only to build upon shifting sands.'

In truth, the Panurge of the *Tiers Livre* and *Quart Livre* is shamefully egoistical. He takes everything that is given him, offers little in return, bends all his actions towards looking after himself first and foremost. He is not so much wicked, as selfish; he offends against the cardinal Rabelaisian precept, love thy neighbours as thyself. Yet Pantagruel forgives him. He knows that there is no wilful evil in the man's nature.

Panurge is also a very bad Christian, that is to say a very

orthodox Christian. He does not pray to God; rather does he plead with the saints and with the Virgin Mary to protect him. His religion is fundamentally superstition and fear. Like the churchmen, he mumbles various formulas whose meaning he does not understand. Salvation for him means being left alone to have fun. Panurge's religion takes no account whatever of morality. What a challenge it is to Pantagruel's evangelism to save this foolish man from himself!

Some of the funniest scenes in the book centre around Panurge. There is, for example, the magnificent virtuoso scene in which Panurge questions a friar, and receives answers only in monosyllables (*Cinquième Livre*, XXVIII). Perhaps the most famous scenes in all Rabelais, known even to those who have never read the book, are those where the sheep follow each other into the sea and drown (*Quart Livre*, VI, VII, VIII), and the scenes of the mighty storm. Panurge is the centre of both.

5. Frère Jean des Entommeures

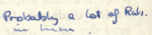
Probably a lot of Rab. in him.

> jeune, guallant, frisque, de hayt, bien à dextre, hardy, adventureux, délibéré, hault, maigre, bien fendu de gueule, bien advantagé en nez, beau despecheur d'heures, beau desbrideur de messes, beau descroteur de vigiles, pour tout dire sommairement vray moyne si oncques en feut depuis le monde moynant moyna de moynerie.
>
> (*Gargantua*, XXVII)

> young, gallant, sprightly, jovial, resourceful, bold, adventurous, resolute, tall, and thin fellow with a great gaping mouth and fine outstanding nose. He was grand mumbler of matins, despatcher of masses, and polisher off of vigils and, to put it briefly, a true monk if ever there has been one since the monking world monked its first monkery.

Ugly, dirty, and profoundly ignorant, Frère Jean has most of the faults common to his fraternity. He freely admits that he

SOME PORTRAITS AND OPINIONS 103

never studied in his monastery, and had no regrets. He knows his prayer-book back to front, but does not understand a word of it. In short, he is the sort of monk whom Rabelais remorselessly criticized.

However, Frère Jean possesses redeeming qualities which lift him far above the mass of friars whose social purposelessness Rabelais most resented. He is courageous, open, honest, and active. He is certainly not lazy:

> Il n'est poinct bigot; il n'est poinct dessiré; il est honeste, joyeux, délibéré, bon compaignon; il travaille; il labeure; il deffent les opprimez; il conforte les affligez; il subvient ès souffreteux; il garde le clou de l'abbaye.
>
> (*Gargantua*, XL)

> He's no bigot, he's no wastrel; he is honest, gay, and resolute, and a good companion; he works, he labours, he defends the oppressed, he comforts the afflicted, he aids the suffering, and he saves the close of his abbey.

Frère Jean is an amusing conversationalist who can tell a good bawdy joke better than anyone. He is marvellous company. His slang and his latinisms are larded with swear-words which he calls 'couleurs de rethorique Cicéroniane'. However filthy his appearance and habits, Frère Jean is infinitely more likeable than Panurge. His friendship and loyalty are unshakeable. While Panurge degenerates into reprehensible cowardice and selfishness, Frère Jean, on the other hand, remains ready at all times to risk his own life in the service of his fellow-men. He is always on hand when disaster threatens, always anxious to help the afflicted. Rabelais wishes to paint in this character the sort of man whose goodness is crushed by the oppressive monastical system, and who could be so useful if the system were improved. It is Frère Jean who conceives the glorious Abbaye de Thélème.

6. Picrochole

Picrochole (and Anarche, whom he resembles) is the very opposite of diplomatic. His qualities are not those required of a politician. Vain, ambitious, impulsive, naïve, violent, his war is a war of conquest and prestige. On learning that one of his men has been attacked, he feels himself personally insulted, and flies into a rage:

> Lequel incontinent entra en courroux furieux, et sans plus oultre se interroguer quoy ne comment, feist crier par son pays ban et arrière ban . . .   (*Gargantua*, XXVI)

> The king promptly flew into a furious rage and, without any further question of why or how, called out his vassals great and small.

His impetuosity causes death and suffering to thousands. Unwilling to listen to reason, he allows himself to be lulled into dreams of empire-building by his unscrupulous advisers. Picrochole has no concept of justice; the generosity of his adversary is simply incomprehensible to his mean and petty mind. Deservedly, he disappears at the end of the war into some obscure and anonymous retreat.

7. The Peasants

Rabelais, born a country boy, understands and sympathizes with the peasantry. He admires their honest toil and labour, their capacity for simple amusements, their loyalty to one another, their frank and serene acceptance of life, their picturesque language. Smiling in the face of adversity, and never complaining, one feels that they are 'the salt of the earth' and would not let one down. 'Les paysans de Rabelais . . . sont de vrais paysans et non des bergers de pastorale.' (Pierre Jourda).

Rabelais's remaining characters are not portrayed with anything like the same depth. They are mostly caricatures, but caricatures which reveal constant acuity of observation. Thus Janotus de Bragmardo (in *Gargantua*), the archetype of the Sorbonne academic, interrupts his tedious ungrammatical speech with nervous habitual coughs; he comes alive in the few pages in which he figures. Thus also the magistrate Grippeminault in the *Cinquième Livre* is not given any specific personality of his own, but his avarice and pedantry are satirized with masterful concision while Bridoye in the *Tiers Livre* is a much more sympathetic character. For the most part, the vast gallery of Rabelaisian characters are types representing the class of sixteenth-century French society from which they are drawn. Together, they constitute a precious social document of the period.

Rabelais achieved immense popularity in his own lifetime. Between 1532, when *Pantagruel* was first put on sale at the Lyon Book Fair, and 1553, when Rabelais died, at least forty-three editions of his works were published. Even more impressively, his popularity has remained at the same high level for the 400 years since his death. Rabelais's achievement is almost unique in this regard.

Nevertheless, while Rabelais has never ceased to be an important figure in the history of French literature, there has been a wide variety of interpretations of his work. No assessment of his contribution to literature has ever been accepted as definitive.

Not many years after Rabelais's death, a near-contemporary, Pierre Boulenger, predicted that he would be 'une énigme pour la postérité'. Subsequent judgements have proved him right. Boulenger himself saw Rabelais as a benevolent moralist in much the same way as Molière would be in the following century: 'un autre Démocrite qui se riait des vaines terreurs, des espérances non moins vaines du vulgaire et des grands de la terre, ainsi que des labeurs anxieux qui remplissent cette courte vie.' (1587). Théophile Gautier had a similar idea in mind when he called Rabelais a 'Homère moqueur'.

The enigma has been particularly trying for those thin-skinned writers who found it difficult to reconcile Rabelais's intellect with his coarseness. While admiring his intelligence, they despise his humour. La Bruyère considered the dilemma insoluble. He invites us to accept two versions of Rabelais, the one admirable, the other lamentable: 'Où il est mauvais, il passe bien loin au-delà du pire, c'est le charme de la canaille; où il est bon il va jusqu'à l'exquis et à l'excellent, il peut être le mets des plus délicats.' Other moralists have been less generous. Lamartine called him quite simply 'le boueux de l'humanité'.

There have been those for whom Rabelais was principally an anti-Christian writer, such as St François de Sales, who spoke of 'l'infâme Rabelais', and, in modern times, Abel Lefranc, who dug deeper than anyone, and discovered a 'pensée secrète' which he identified as the most militant atheism of the sixteenth century. One modern critic has even revealed a communist Rabelais. Henri Lefebvre says that 'l'idéal thélémite sert de transition entre le communisme primitif et le communisme scientifique'. This same writer thinks that Frère Jean des Entommeures is meant to be Joan of Arc.

Fanciful interpretations such as these derive from the concern to take literally Rabelais's own advice to his reader, that he should not be fooled by the apparent frivolity of the story, but should break the bone and 'sugcer la sustantificque moelle'. Rabelais would have been the first to admit that he did not intend us to look so deeply that we find hidden messages which are not there. He is simply saying, in the famous preface, that his intention is as much satirical as farcical; but the objects of the satire are self-evident, and do not have to be sought with a geiger-counter. Rabelais does not mystify us with symbols.

It is just as easy to fall into the opposite trap, that of taking the legend seriously and seeing in Rabelais no more than an author 'simplement plaisans' (Montaigne). Rabelais did, it is true, advertise his drunkenness and often leave the reader with a crafty smile which warned him not to take the stories too seriously. But such a point of view cannot possibly be maintained on the evidence of the books themselves. It is sheer obstinacy to perpetuate the myth and say, with Voltaire, that Rabelais is 'un philosophe ivre qui n'a écrit que dans le temps de son ivresse'. 'Il n'y a que quelques personnes d'un goût bizarre,' continues Voltaire, 'qui se piquent d'entendre et d'estimer tout cet ouvrage; le reste de la nation rit des plaisanteries de Rabelais et méprise le livre.' And that prolific nineteenth-century critic Émile Faguet offers the most haughty dismissal of a great writer that is to be found in the annals of French literary criticism. Having stated that it is a mistake to seek any sort of message in Rabelais's stories, he writes: 'c'est un esprit de village français ... qui ne manque pas de saveur du reste pour les lecteurs au-dessous de douze ans ... Tel me paraît être cet homme très peu singulier, très peu mystérieux et même assez peu profond, qui a eu ce seul mérite, mais assez rare, d'être à la fois un homme de bon sens et un homme d'imagination.' One wonders just how much of the five books Faguet has read.

On the whole, however, Rabelais has generally been regarded as the father of French literature. Victor Hugo called him 'un des gouffres de l'esprit', and Jean Cocteau has gone on record as saying that 'Rabelais, ce sont les entrailles de la France'.

Pierre Jourda has written the following: 'C'est un art tumultueux que l'art de Rabelais; on dirait d'un fleuve qui roule à gros bouillons, entraînant tout dans son cours, et charriant parfois plus de boue que d'eau claire. Mais, dans sa surabondance, c'est un art sûr de ses moyens et de ses effets ... La verve y domine plus que la méthode, une verve saine, joyeuse et robuste ...' And he continues, speaking of *Gargantua*, 'c'est le premier chef-d'oeuvre de la prose française. . . . Avec lui commence la littérature française moderne et s'affirme pleinement, dans sa fougue parfois outrancière, l'essor de la Renaissance.'[1] Few nowadays would disagree.

The final word belongs to Chateaubriand, who described François Rabelais as 'un des génies-mères de l'humanité'.

il a créé les lettres françaises.

[1] Pierre Jourda, op. cit., pp. 84, 87.

Bibliography

P. Stapfer, *Rabelais, sa personne, son génie et son oeuvre*, Paris, 1899.

P. Villey, *Marot et Rabelais*, Paris, 1923.

A. France, *Rabelais*, in *Oeuvre Complètes*, XVII, Paris, 1929.

J. Plattard, *État présent des études rabelaisiennes*, Paris, 1927.

J. Plattard, *La Vie de François Rabelais*, Paris, 1932.

J. Plattard, *La Vie et L'Oeuvre de Rabelais*, Paris, 1939 and 1952.

L. Febvre, *Le Problème de l'Incroyance au XVIe siècle; la Religion de Rabelais*, Paris, 1942.

P. Jourda, *Le Gargantua de Rabelais*, Paris, 1948.

A. Lefranc, *Études sur Gargantua, Pantagruel, le Tiers Livre*, Paris, 1953, reprinted from introductions to Champion editions, 1912, 1922.

H. Lefebvre, *Rabelais*, Paris, 1955.

E. Gilson, *Rabelais franciscain*, Paris, 1955.

V.-L. Saulnier, *Le Dessein de Rabelais*, Paris, 1957.

A. J. Krailsheimer, *Rabelais*, Paris, 1967.

M. A. Screech, *L'Évangélisme de Rabelais*, Geneva, 1959.

M. de Diéguez, *Rabelais par lui-même*, Paris, 1960.

A. J. Krailsheimer, *Rabelais and the Franciscans*, Oxford, 1963.

E. Faguet, *XVIe Siècle*.

M. A. Screech, *The Rabelaisian Marriage*, London, 1958.